The Canoe Shop

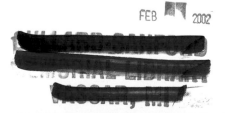

CHRIS KULCZYCKI

The Canoe Shop

Three Elegant Wooden Canoes
Anyone Can Build

RAGGED MOUNTAIN PRESS/MCGRAW-HILL
Camden, Maine • New York • Chicago • San Francisco
• Lisbon • London • Madrid • Mexico City • Milan • New Delhi
• San Juan • Seoul • Singapore • Sydney • Toronto

Ragged Mountain Press

A Division of The McGraw·Hill Companies

10 9 8 7 6 5 4 3 2 1

Copyright © 2001 Chris Kulczycki

All rights reserved. The publisher takes no responsibility for the use of any of the materials or methods described in this book, nor for the products thereof. The name "Ragged Mountain Press" and the Ragged Mountain Press logo are trademarks of The McGraw-Hill Companies. Printed in the United States of America.

Library of Congress Cataloging-in-Publication Data
Kulczycki, Chris, 1958–
    The canoe shop : three elegant wooden canoes anyone can build / Chris Kulczycki.
              p.   cm.
Includes index.
ISBN 0-07-137227-X
    1. Canoes and canoeing. 2. Boatbuilding. I. Title.

VM353.K8497 2001
623.8′29—dc21   00-012862

Questions regarding the content of this book should be addressed to
Ragged Mountain Press
P.O. Box 220
Camden, ME 04843
www.raggedmountainpress.com

Questions regarding the ordering of this book should be addressed to
The McGraw-Hill Companies
Customer Service Department
P.O. Box 547
Blacklick, OH 43004
Retail customers: 1-800-262-4729
Bookstores: 1-800-722-4726

This book is printed on 70# Citation by R. R. Donnelley, Crawfordsville, IN
Design by Shannon Swanson
Production management and page layout by Janet Robbins
Edited by Jonathan Eaton, Alex Barnett, and Allen Gooch
All illustrations by John C. Harris
All photos courtesy the author

Amana Tools, Brightside, Cab-O-Sil, CMT, Dacron, Epifanes, Freud, Interlux, Kevlar, LapStitch, Lexus, Lufkin, MAS, Microlight, Popsicle, Porter Cable, Shelman, Starrett Tools, 3M, West System, Wen, and Z-Spar are registered trademarks.

WARNING: Building and maintaining a boat can expose you to potentially dangerous situations and substances. Reference to brand names does not indicate endorsement of or guarantee the safety of using these products. In using this book, the reader releases the author, publisher, and distributor from liability for any loss or injury, including death, allegedly caused, in whole or in part, by relying on information contained in this book.

for Alec

▶Contents

▶ACKNOWLEDGMENTS

Annette Najjar is my editor, critic, and loving wife. She encourages, assists, and pulls no punches. She is a dynamo, and I doubt if anything around here, this book included, would get done without her.

The boatbuilder in the photos is my friend Bill Thomas. In addition to being a first-rate professional boatbuilder, Bill is a master cabinetmaker and a fellow instructor at the WoodenBoat School in Maine. The photographs were taken in Bill's shop in Columbia, South Carolina. He's built many of my boats, including a number of Sassafras canoes for his customers. While I was visiting to photograph this book, Bill and I spent several pleasant evenings sitting on his porch talking about the building process and working out various shortcuts and improvements that have been incorporated into the instructions. Since Bill's porch overlooks a lovely pond, we were also able to take turns in the Sassafras 14 he keeps on its bank. It was nice to see one of my designs perform so well in the hands of an expert canoeist.

John Harris drew the plans and sketches in this book. In addition to being a skilled draftsman, John is a fine boatbuilder and a talented designer.

I first paddled a canoe at the age of eight. My mother had taken a temporary job as nurse at a girls' summer camp, and I went along. Had I been a few years older, other recreational opportunities might have occurred to me. But for an eight-year-old from the city, catching snakes and turtles, fishing, and learning to canoe were more interesting than girl campers. I remember dragging a heavy aluminum canoe across a wide beach and paddling along the bank of a muddy lake full of bluegills and snapping turtles, struggling to go in a straight line and to reach a distant cove. My tiny arms ached as I tacked across the lake.

The following year my parents bought a cabin near the Shenandoah River, and it was back to canoes. After several summers at the cabin, I could paddle a canoe well enough, both on flatwater and whitewater. But I never got over the feeling that most canoes are simply too big and heavy.

Thirty years later my wife and I moved to a waterfront home near Chesapeake Bay, and I started canoeing again. Now a professional boat designer, I'd started Chesapeake Light Craft Inc., a company that soon became the largest boat-kit manufacturer in the world. So I decided to design a series of small, light, easy-to-build, and pretty wooden canoes, canoes that looked and handled the way I thought a canoe should.

Although my company would offer precut kits for these canoes, I intended that they also could be built from scratch by novice woodworkers. Having designed many popular kayaks, rowing boats, and even a few sailboats, I thought designing canoes would be easy. But what almost stopped the canoe project was the lack of a suitable building method; methods that were fast and simple resulted in slow, homely boats, while traditional building techniques required more skill and time than I thought the average amateur woodworker could muster. Eventually I came up with the LapStitch method, which combines the beauty and light weight of lapstrake boatbuilding with the speed and ease of a modern construction method called stitch-and-glue boatbuilding. This new method allows novice builders to create canoes that, I believe, are as good as any made today.

The Canoe Shop

CHAPTER ONE

▶*Building Canoes*

Together we'll build a wooden canoe. I'll provide the plans and instructions; you'll furnish the materials and muscle. Our canoe will be light, strong, stiff, and a joy to paddle. It'll be simple to build; anyone with even a modicum of woodworking skill and a few free weekends can complete one. No expensive power tools will be required, and though the materials used might not be found in every town, they can be ordered from a boatbuilder's catalog and shipped anywhere. And all the plans and instructions you'll need are right here in front of you.

The Sassafras Canoes

I designed the Sassafras canoes for flatwater paddling, for fishing, camping, and nature photography, and for just getting out on the water with a special friend. I live on a creek that empties a few hundred yards downstream into a wide river, which, 3 miles down, flows into Chesapeake Bay. Off this river, and dozens like it on the Chesapeake, branch many

creeks that wind through marshland and forest and that are perfect for canoeing. Sometimes I take along my fly rod, though the perch and striped bass have little to fear from me.

Although the Sassafras canoes are designed primarily for our flat and tranquil creeks, a nasty chop can build on the river, and my canoes must be able to get me home. But, please understand, even though they can handle some waves, these are not whitewater boats. They may

The Sassafras canoes have simple lines and a conservative design.

The Sassafras 12 is a solo canoe that can be paddled with a double or kayak paddle, or a traditional canoe paddle.

survive the occasional encounter with a rock or log, but serious rock bashing in rapids will damage them. Canoes designed for ease of paddling on quiet water don't have the maneuverability or strength required in rapids.

There are three versions of the Sassafras: a 12-foot solo canoe, a 14-foot solo or two-person version, and the 16-foot tandem (actually 15 feet, 8 inches). All three are light enough to be hoisted onto a car's roof rack by one person. And carrying them to the water is no chore, which guarantees that they'll get plenty of use.

The 14-footer makes a fine solo canoe.

Bill and Ansley Thomas enjoy the Sassafras 14.

Like many traditional canoes, the Sassafras models have a symmetrical bow and stern. This design allows a solo paddler in the 14- and 16-footers to sit facing "backward" on the forward seat for better trim. This also makes these canoes easier to build, as you'll soon discover. All three versions have good initial stability; they don't feel too tippy. More important, they have great secondary stability; that is, they can be leaned far over before they capsize. But the Sassafras canoes are not as stable as low-end beginner boats, which you'd soon outgrow. Their slightly rounded hulls offer more speed and responsiveness than many of the plastic or fiberglass boats you

The Sassafras 16 moves easily, even with only one paddler.

may have paddled. The hulls are slightly rockered, or curved along the keel. This is not for maneuvering in whitewater, but rather for reducing wetted-surface area—making for almost effortless paddling. You'll find that these boats have a smooth, stiff, and solid feel that's characteristic of all good wooden canoes. And, like all lapstrake craft, they make a wonderful gurgling sound as they move through still water.

These canoes are a little smaller than is traditional. Today we carry lighter loads; when did you last bring home a quartered moose or paddle into town for flour, salt, and a barrel of gunpowder? I think their sizes make these canoes easier to paddle and to turn because of lower wetted-surface area, and the smaller size certainly makes them lighter.

How Canoes Are Built

We know that the first canoes were dugouts, built from logs hollowed out by fire and primitive tools. Later, native North Americans perfected the birchbark canoe. European explorers introduced lapstrake canoes, wood and canvas canoes, and strip-built canoes.

Today, most wooden canoes are built using the strip method. The builder first makes molds and a strongback, which resemble a boat's frame and define its shape. Thin strips of wood are stapled or tacked to the molds and glued to each other. In the past, many thin frames reinforced the hull, but today fiberglass and epoxy are used instead. When the glue dries, the sta-

Lapstrake and LapStitch canoes have overlapping planks that give them a sleek and elegant appearance.

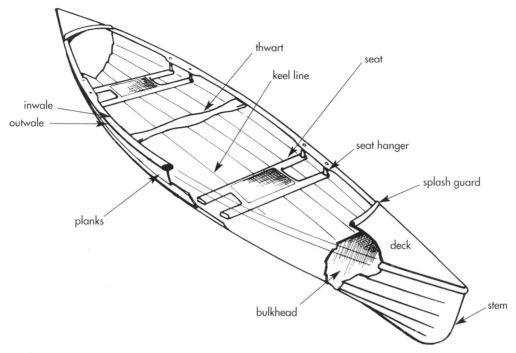

A lapstrake canoe in cross section.

ples are removed and the hull is covered with fiberglass cloth set in epoxy; then it is lifted off the molds. Finally, the inside is sheathed with fiberglass and the gunwales, seats, thwart, and trim are added.

Some paddlers think that all wooden canoes are strip-built, but lapstrake, or *clinker*, canoes have a long history. The lapstrake method uses wider planks, or *strakes*, that overlap like the siding on a house. This was the method used to build Viking longboats and most of the working craft in Northern Europe. When colonists tried to improve on the Native Americans' birchbark and dugout canoes, they naturally turned to lapstrake construction. Many of the fabled Rushton canoes were lapstrake, and these models were often the lightest and most beautiful. The famous Rob Roy canoe was lapstrake, as

was George W. Sears's 10-pound Sairy Gamp.

Lapstrake construction is, to my eye at least, the most beautiful way to build a boat. The overlapping strakes, and particularly the shadows cast by them, accentuate the graceful lines of a handsome hull. Traditionally, the strakes were nailed or riveted together and reinforced with frames. With the advent of epoxy they could be glued, making for very stiff but light hulls. Innovative builders, particularly Vermonter Tom Hill, specialized in and popularized modern ultralight lapstrake canoes.

Of course, most lapstrake boats are built on a strongback and molds by boatbuilders of considerable skill; they are certainly not projects for novice woodworkers. Actually, all the construction methods mentioned require a fair bit of joinery skill. The strips in a strip boat must be cut to a perfect fit; the strakes in a lapstrake hull must be carefully shaped and beveled where they meet. But even before building the boat, the builder must fabricate the strongback and molds, and that can take almost as long as building the boat. Even building a birchbark canoe demands considerable knowledge and skill. There had to be an easier way, and I set out to find it.

LapStitch Construction

The company I founded, Chesapeake Light Craft, has had considerable success manufacturing and marketing computer-designed boat plans and kits for amateur

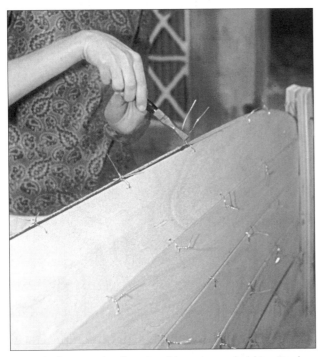

Instead of a strongback and molds, wire ties hold LapStitch boats together until they are glued.

construction. In fact, when I sold the company in 1999, it was the largest manufacturer of kit boats in the world. Our specialty was small boats that could be built without strongbacks and molds. Using sophisticated software, I designed boats that would require minimal frames and interior structure. Using this same software, I determined the exact three-dimensional shape of all the parts of the boat and then *expanded* them to view their shapes when they are flat—that is, I "unbent" the planks after the design was completed to establish each plank's flat shape.

With the expanded shapes of all the parts established, they would be cut from mahogany plywood and joined using the *stitch-and-glue* method of boatbuilding. The stitch-and-glue method entails temporarily joining the parts at their edges with short twists of copper wire, thus holding the boat in shape without need of strongbacks and molds and frames. When the precisely cut flat panels are stitched up and joined, they bend to form the exact shape of the boat I'd designed. Next, the panels are glued with epoxy and fiberglass.

The resulting boats are almost as strong as fiberglass boats but lighter and far prettier. Someone with virtually no woodworking experience can build them; after all, the shape of the planks is right there in the plans—all you have to do is cut them out and join them at the edges (or join the precut panels in a kit). This is the technique I wanted to apply to building lapstrake canoes.

The problem was that complex rolling bevels are required at the edge of each plank of a lapstrake boat. This is

The traditional lapstrake joint.

The LapStitch joint in cross section.

what made the boats too difficult for novice woodworkers to tackle. Finally, I hit upon the idea of cutting a *rabbet*, or groove, on the bottom of each strake so that it fits right over the strake below. This groove would be filled with epoxy, eliminating the need for the bevels and precisely aligned planks. Using this technique, the hull is stitched together like a stitch-and-glue boat, the seams filled with epoxy, and the interior components installed soon after. As a bonus, much less epoxy and fiberglass work is required than in a typical stitch-and-glue boat because the plank laps do not require many fillets or much fiberglass reinforcement. It is this new LapStitch construction method that allows the Sassafras canoes to be built so quickly and easily.

It's difficult to believe that no one had thought up the LapStitch method be-

fore now. The U.S. Patent Office, however, determined that this was a novel idea and I was awarded a patent for a "Method for Building Lapstrake Boats" in November 2000.

Building Your Own Canoe

The Canoe Shop is written for novice woodworkers. It's easier for you experts to skip the rudimentary woodworking advice than it is for beginners to find expert help. So, old pros, remember what it was like when you were just starting out, and bear with us. I've taught over 30 weeklong boatbuilding classes and I have a good idea what questions to expect. And I did try to cover them all, but no doubt you will think up new ones. Many of your questions will be answered if you read through the

Most of the photos in this book were taken in Bill Thomas's idyllic shop. Bill builds fine custom boats for customers all over the country.

entire book before you start building.

It's interesting that the best wood-workers don't always build the best boats. I've had several professional cabinetmakers in my classes who thought they could im-prove on designs and on established boat-building methods; I have yet to see one succeed, at least on the first try. Many first-time builders don't realize how much experience and time goes into designing a boat. A lawyer enrolled in one of my courses announced after the first day of class that this was great fun, and when he retired he might become a professional boatbuilder and designer. I agreed that it was a splendid idea; perhaps I would open a law office when I retired.

Often, my students who have little woodworking skill, but who are resolute in precisely following directions and in taking their time, build the best boats. Boatbuilding is a contemplative and meticulous endeavor. Slow down, think each step through, look at the plans once again, reread the instructions, and you'll soon have a fine canoe.

The canoe shown in most of the con-struction photographs in this book is the Sassafras 16, but the two smaller versions are built in the same way. Where there are minor construction differences, they're noted in the text and on the plans repro-duced in chapter 4.

CHAPTER TWO

▶*The Materials*

Sassafras canoes aren't wooden boats in the traditional sense; they're more accurately described as wood-epoxy composite construction. Marine-grade mahogany plywood is used instead of solid wood. This construction method makes finding and milling the wood for our craft far simpler than for traditional boatbuilding. Epoxy and fiberglass are substituted for traditional fasteners and coatings, giving these boats many of the qualities we associate with modern plastics: strength, durability, and resistance to corrosion and rot.

The design of the Sassafras canoes doesn't allow for much choice in the selection of materials. It requires top-quality wood and the best epoxy resin. Using inferior materials will result in an unsatisfactory craft.

Plywood

The Sassafras canoes should be built from marine-grade *okoume* plywood. Okoume is a light but strong African mahogany. It's fairly soft for a hardwood, making it easy to work with hand tools. It's also an attractive wood, light brown with an occasional bit of red and enough variation in the grain to form interesting patterns. Some sheets of okoume plywood have beautiful swirling grain, dark streaks, or a burled appearance. Okoume is grown in West African–managed forests and plantations. Most logs are shipped to Europe, where a handful of mills manufacture the plywood. Although many woodworkers have never heard of okoume, it's a common boatbuilding material.

You might think the reason to use exotic, and expensive, marine plywood is to ensure the glue used between the *plies*, or layers, is waterproof. But today almost all glue used in plywood panels is waterproof. The real difference between marine- and construction-grade plywood is the quality of the individual plies. Marine-grade plywood doesn't, or shouldn't, contain *voids*, or gaps, in the inner layers. Because the plywood will be bent as it's shaped into a boat, it's likely to snap at a void. Even if the panel doesn't break during construction, the void will cause a weak spot that may crack when your canoe hits a rock or log.

Furniture-grade plywood, or *lauan* plywood, may have nice veneers on the surface, but the core plies are likely to be weak filler wood. You'll also notice that the surface plies in marine plywood are fairly thick. Furniture-grade plywood will have very thin face veneers since they are there for the sake of appearance, not for strength. When the plywood panel is bent, it is those surface plies that are most important for strength.

Mahogany plywood is graded using the British Standards system, not the A-B-C grades you're probably familiar with. The panels for your canoe should be stamped "BS1088" or British Standard 10.88; this is the highest standard. There is a surprising difference in quality even among BS1088 panels; I wonder whether panels from some mills actually meet the standard. Buy your plywood only from distributors with the best reputations. I've been most impressed by Shelman-brand plywood, made by a Swiss-owned mill in Greece. Fortunately, Shelman has a huge mill and its wood is relatively easy to find in many parts of the world. You may also encounter okoume plywood that's made to Lloyd's of London specifications; usually such plywood also meets BS1088. Okoume plywood that's stamped BS6566 is exterior-grade plywood that may have very thin face veneers and may contain voids—don't use it for these canoes. Often Okoume plywood is metric sized (250 by 125 cm), which is a little larger than a standard 4- by 8-foot sheet of domestic plywood.

Because okoume plywood is relatively expensive, I am often asked about cheaper alternatives. Frankly, for high-quality small boats, the only alternatives are other species of African mahogany such as marine-grade *khaya* and *sapele*, which are even more expensive. I know that a few amateur boatbuilders use lauan or fir exterior-grade plywood for their hulls. Unless a boat is designed specifically to be built from exterior-grade plywood, however, using these types of wood is a potentially dangerous practice because of the voids and very thin face veneers. Exterior-grade panels also take far more time to finish than the better marine grades, so you'll lose in time what you'll have saved in cost. Finally, consider that marine-grade plywood panels are less than half the cost of the materials used in most boats. If an inexpensive panel fails, you'll have wasted not only the plywood but also a lot of expensive fiberglass, epoxy, and other materials.

Plywood should be stamped BS1088 or British Standard 10.88.

All domestic marine-grade plywood is made from Douglas fir. Douglas fir is a superb solid wood—light, strong, and durable. Unfortunately, it makes poor plywood for canoe hulls because it's prone to *checking*, or splitting. The nature of fir and the quality standards of American plywood manufacturers combine to make this plywood unattractive and difficult to finish.

Solid Wood

In a Sassafras canoe, only the gunwales, seats, thwart, and deck trim are made from solid wood. I usually fashion all these parts from ash, white oak, or mahogany, though the inwales might be of softwood such as cypress, white cedar, spruce, or fir to save weight. I prefer trim of a contrasting color. Since okoume is a light- to medium-brown color when varnished, woods like light-colored ash or dark Honduran mahogany provide a striking accent. But most strong, straight-grained wood you might have in your shop will do. I do avoid teak since its color is too close to that of okoume; teak is also difficult to glue and very expensive. A few types of wood, including poplar and birch, are not good choices because they tend to stain and turn black when exposed to water.

It's easiest to buy a single board the length of your canoe from which to rip the gunwales. A single ¾-inch by 8-inch by 16-foot board will yield all the solid wood parts for any of these canoes. If you can't find a suitably long board, short sections can be joined with a scarf joint.

Epoxy

LapStitch boats must be built using marine epoxy adhesives. Epoxy is a plastic that starts out as two liquid components: *resin* and *hardener*. When the resin and hardener are mixed to the proper ratio, they harden, or *cure*, into a tough clear solid. Other resins and glues also cure to a tough solid, but their adhesive qualities are not nearly strong enough to hold the planks together. The common fiberglassing resin, which is polyester resin, will not work, nor will vinylester resin. If you are considering using one of these less-expensive adhesives, close your eyes, imagine paddling your new canoe on a beautiful lake and suddenly hearing a resounding "sproing!" Now imagine swimming to shore.

The ratio of resin to hardener varies among brands of epoxy. It's critical that epoxy be mixed precisely to the manufacturer's instructions. Epoxy that has too much, or too little, hardener will not achieve full strength when cured, or it may not cure at all. If you've used polyester resins, you're familiar with catalyst, a few drops of which cause the resin to harden. The hardener used with epoxy does not work in the same way. Think of it as part of the plastic: one molecule of hardener must meet with and join one molecule of the resin. Extra molecules won't find a mate and solidify, they'll just float around weakening the mixture. Increasing the amount of hardener will not cause faster curing, but it will result in a much weaker bond.

Because epoxy resin and hardener

The epoxy station in Bill's shop has everything close at hand. The floodlight keeps the epoxy resin warm so it flows easily; cold resin will thicken and clog the metering pump.

Epoxy is thinner than most glue; it'll flow out of gaps and joints unless it's first mixed with a *thickening agent*, or *filler*. When reading instructions, be sure to distinguish between hardener and thickener. Hardener is a liquid that is always mixed into the resin, whereas thickener is a powder, which is added only for some applications. Remember that thickeners don't have any chemical effect on the mix; they simply make the epoxy thicker.

Epoxy manufacturers sell many types of thickening agents for various applications. I suggest using *silica powder* (such as Cab-O-Sil) or *silica fibers* for gluing scarfs and other tight joints. Use *wood flour* for making *fillets*, or beads of thick epoxy paste. Microballoons are microscopic hollow glass or plastic spheres. They are mixed with epoxy to make a very light and easily sanded paste for filling imperfections.

The amount of thickener added to the epoxy varies with the application. Here are five recipes that will cover any epoxy use in LapStitch boatbuilding.

- When filling seams between the strakes, use epoxy slightly thickened with silica to the consistency of thin gravy. The mix should flow easily, since you'll be using a syringe to apply it.
- When coating, sealing, or saturating wood with epoxy, don't add any thickening powder. You'll also use this unthickened mixture to saturate fiberglass cloth and tape.
- When joining wood to wood, add enough silica powder to the resin/hardener mix to bring it to the consistency of mayonnaise or

are thick and sticky, using cups to measure them is both inaccurate and unpleasant. Most epoxy manufacturers sell inexpensive plastic pumps designed to overcome the mixing problem. These *calibrated metering pumps* look like the pumps you've seen in large jugs of ketchup. They screw into the tops of the resin and hardener containers and precisely meter the liquids. The resin and hardener will be dispensed at the exact ratio required, and you'll only need to stir them thoroughly.

When using calibrated pumps, you push only one stroke for the resin and one stroke for the hardener. Do not push the resin and hardener pumps to the manufacturer's stated ratio, say, two pushes of resin to one push of hardener if the manufacturer's ratio is 2:1. If mixing in a measuring cup, you would use this ratio, but because these pumps are calibrated, you push each pump only once.

jam. Let the mix sit on the joint for a minute or two before clamping. You'll use this mixture for gluing scarf joints and on the inwales and outwales.

- For making a fillet or filling a gap, add sufficient wood flour to make a smooth peanut butter–like paste. This mixture is used to strengthen joints and seams.

- To fill imperfections and smooth rough areas, make a light paste by adding microballoons to the epoxy. Microballoon paste is not particularly strong and should not be used as glue or for structural fillets. Some builders won't bother with microballoons; instead, they fill scratches and wire holes with wood flour and epoxy and spend a few more minutes sanding.

It is very important to mix the epoxy and hardener thoroughly before adding thickener, then to mix again after adding it—one epoxy manufacturer estimates that improper mixing causes 90 percent of epoxy problems. Stir epoxy vigorously for a full minute—look at your watch—before using or adding thickening powder.

Because epoxy is readily absorbed by wood, it will affect the wood's bending properties. So it's important to wipe up any epoxy that oozes out of joints before it can harden. It's also important not to "starve" the joints. If too little epoxy is used, it will all be absorbed by the wood, leaving a joint that is dry and weak. If a joint is to be clamped, let the epoxy sit on the wood for a few minutes to determine whether more is needed before joining the

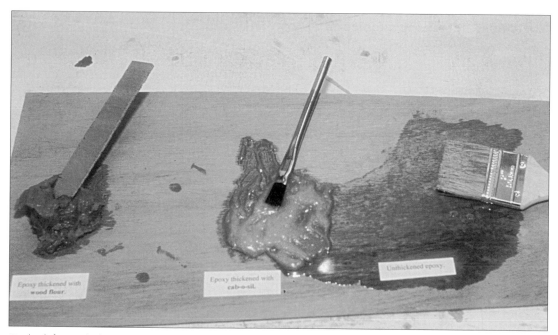

Epoxy thickened with wood flour.

Epoxy thickened with cab-o-sil.

Unthickened epoxy.

To the left is a thick mixture made with wood flour used in fillets and for filling gaps. Next is epoxy mixed with silica powder for gluing wood-to-wood joints. On the right is clear epoxy, as you would use for coating.

parts permanently. Don't apply any more clamping pressure than is necessary to make a tight joint, or you'll squeeze out all the epoxy.

Before recoating epoxy, check for *amine blush*, a waxy film that can form on the surface of some epoxy. If the surface feels slightly wet or greasy, amine blush is present. It must be cleaned off before recoating to obtain a strong bond between epoxy coats. Amine blush is water-soluble; use soapy water and a scrub pad to remove it. Some brands of epoxy, notably MAS epoxy when used with its slow hardener, do not form blush. When recoating epoxy that has cured for more than 48 hours, sand the surface lightly first to roughen it. This ensures a good mechanical bond. Freshly cured epoxy forms a strong chemical bond to a fresh coat over it, but as the epoxy continues to harden, a mechanical bond is required. So it's best to overcoat within 48 hours, as no surface preparation will then be required.

Many companies market marine epoxy systems consisting of various resins, hardeners, thickeners, and application tools. Some of these brands are too thick to flow into the tight seams required in LapStitch construction. Others are prone to producing amine blush. I've had particularly good results with MAS and West System brands.

The minimum temperature for working with most epoxies is about 60°F, but if you require cure times of less than 24 hours and are using slow hardener, a temperature of higher than 70°F is needed. Fast hardeners are available for use in cool weather or for those of you in a hurry. With a few brands of epoxy, it's possible to use a combination of fast and slow hardeners to balance working time and cure time, but most manufacturers advise against mixing their hardeners; be sure to check. MAS offers an unusual epoxy called "Cool Cure." This resin and hardener is specifically formulated for use in unheated or underheated shops and is reported to cure in temperatures as low as 45°F.

As epoxy cures, it generates heat, which accelerates the cure time. A large mass of epoxy left to cure in a container, such as a mixing cup, will harden very rapidly, often in a matter of minutes. But the same quantity of epoxy quickly spread out, as when coating a boat's hull, may take hours to harden. In the first instance, there is relatively little surface area, so the heat generated is not dissipated; this causes the epoxy to solidify rapidly. Conversely, the thin film of epoxy, with much more surface area, allows the heat to dissipate. When long working times are important, always get the epoxy out of the mixing container quickly. A useful technique is to pour the epoxy into a shallow bowl or pie tin to increase working time. Containers of rapidly curing epoxy can generate a significant amount of heat. They may actually boil, producing odorous and unhealthy "epoxy steam." It's good boatshop etiquette to always place leftover mixed epoxy outdoors to harden.

In addition to the resin, hardener, and thickeners you'll need some supplies and tools for working with epoxy. Foremost are dispensing pumps, disposable mixing cups

EPOXY SAFETY

Epoxy resins and hardeners and the solvents used to clean up epoxy spills and tools all contain potentially dangerous chemicals. Follow these simple safety rules and always read the warnings from the epoxy or solvent manufacturer.

- Avoid getting epoxy on your skin; wear disposable gloves and be neat when you work. Continual contact with epoxy can lead to sensitization—you may develop an allergy to epoxy and will never be able to work with it again.

- Although you may clean tools and spills with acetone or lacquer thinner, don't use solvents to remove epoxy from your skin. Solvents can actually drive the chemical into your skin. Instead, use soap and water, vinegar, or, best of all, auto mechanic's waterless hand cleaner.

- Unlike polyester or vinylester resins, epoxy has little odor, but you should still wear a dust mask or respirator when sanding it.

- Avoid breathing dust from thickeners, particularly silica-based powders—this is essentially powdered glass.

- Although epoxy is not particularly flammable, acetone and other solvents used for cleanup are very volatile. Keep them away from open flames and space heaters.

- Always read, and heed, the instructions and warnings on the epoxy container and in other literature provided by the manufacturer.

such as paper cups, yogurt containers, or clean tin cans, and stirring sticks. For applying epoxy, get syringes, disposable bristle brushes, foam rollers, and a plastic squeegee or plastic putty knife. A soupspoon makes a good tool for applying fillets. When coating large, flat areas, use a yellow no-lint foam roller: cut a full-width roller cover in half and use it on a 3-inch roller frame.

You'll also need some fiberglass cloth, which will be set in epoxy to reinforce the bottom of the canoe. Buy 50-inch-wide, 6-ounce E-glass; its length should be the same as the canoe's overall length.

One last tip about working with epoxy: the stuff is unbelievably gooey and sticky, and once it hardens, it's impossible to remove from clothes, carpet, and furniture. "Work clean," as we say in boatbuilding shops.

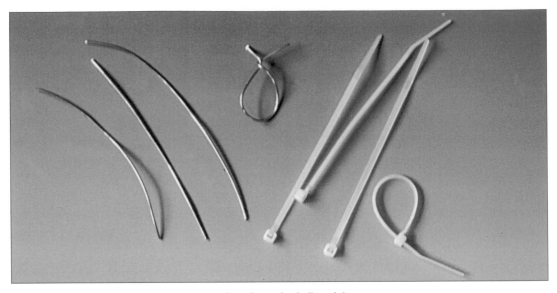

Copper wire or electrical wire ties are used to clamp the hull until the epoxy sets.

Fasteners

Very few metal fasteners are used in a Sassafras canoe, only a few screws and some copper wire. All fasteners, other than the wire, should be of stainless steel or silicon bronze. Stainless steel comes in various grades, some of which are not very stainless at all. So, particularly if you'll be paddling in salt water, buy your screws from a reputable marine dealer. Don't substitute brass fasteners for bronze or stainless steel. They are neither as strong nor as corrosion-resistant.

The other metal fastener you will use is uninsulated copper wire for stitching the hull together. I prefer 18-gauge wire that in past years was sold at many hardware stores for hanging birdfeeders and tying up roses. Today, bare copper wire can be hard to find, and you may need to order it from a marine or boatbuilder's supply house. Copper is the best type of wire to use because it's easy to cut, twist, and sand flush with the wood. Stainless steel wire is available, but it's very stiff, hard to twist, and very difficult to sand. Another option is the plastic ties used to secure electrical wiring. These are inexpensive and available at any electronics or electrical supply house. The smallest size will pass through a ⅛-inch hole; that's bigger than the ¹⁄₁₆-inch hole required for copper wire, but if the boat is to be painted inside and out, the holes can be filled with epoxy putty.

Finding Materials

Asking for okoume plywood at most lumberyards will result in little more than a bewildered salesperson. Marine plywood, epoxies, and fasteners are specialty items. If you don't live in a traditional boatbuilding area, you'll probably have to order at least some of your materials by mail. Ask local boatbuilders where they buy materials or look through the ads in *WoodenBoat* magazine for local sources. There's a list of suppliers who sell by mail in appendix 2.

Buy solid wood from a dedicated lumber dealer, not from a home-improvement store. Every larger town and city has a shop that sells hardwood to cabinetmakers, furniture makers, boat-builders, and high-end homebuilders. Often these lumberyards are found in some industrial ghetto, which is why you may not know about them; ask around. Most lumber dealers have on-site milling facilities and can rip your inwales and outwales if you don't have access to a table saw.

CHAPTER THREE

▶*The Tools*

If you're familiar with traditional boat-building, you'll be surprised by how few tools are required to build these canoes. The tools that you do need, however, should be of the best quality. It's not surprising that boatbuilders take inordinate pride in their tools. A boat's parts, particularly the planks, must be precisely cut and shaped if they are to fit properly. The many curves and odd angles are difficult enough to cut with fine tools; it would be foolish to handicap yourself with cheap, dull, or rusty tools. High-quality tools last longer, work smoother, are easier to use, and can be repaired.

The best advice I can give to someone buying boatbuilding tools is to learn about the tools before you start shopping and then buy the best ones you can afford. It's wiser to get a few top-quality tools than a shop full of consumer-grade tools. And consider that fine tools are a "lifetime" investment. Most of us will need only one drill, one rabbet plane, and one carpenter's square during our lives—if we buy good ones, that is. It's likely that our grandchildren could use those same tools long after we're gone. That's why today's boatbuilders haunt used tool shops, searching for 50-year-old gems used by earlier builders and sold off by estates and uninformed offspring. In fact, a used tool store is one of the best places to buy hand tools—the quality and design of old hand tools, particularly planes, often exceed that of modern versions. As my dear old grandmother used to say, "Only rich people can afford to buy cheap things."

Tool List

ESSENTIAL TOOLS

- Small handsaw
- Rabbet plane (if you have a router, any small, sharp plane will do)
- Drill and bits
- Tape measure
- 12- or 18-inch ruler
- 24-inch carpenter's square
- Chalkline
- Batten
- Protractor or bevel gauge
- Sharp pencils or a mechanical pencil

- C-clamps (at least 12)
- 3 spring clamps
- Pliers
- Diagonal-type wire cutters
- Screwdrivers
- Utility knife
- Rubber sanding block
- Safety glasses
- Dust mask or respirator

OPTIONAL TOOLS

These tools are convenient to have, but don't buy them if it means scrimping on the quality of your essential tools. I've listed them in order of usefulness.

- Saber saw and/or trim saw
- Small sander
- Router and bits
- File
- More clamps
- Table saw

- Keyhole saw
- Marking gauge
- Chisels

Saws

Most of the parts for our canoes can be cut with handsaws. Both Bill and I prefer Japanese-style saws. Many westerners don't realize that Japanese woodworkers were, and are, among the finest in the world. And they've developed superb hand tools that are quite different from their European counterparts.

In some cases the Japanese styles are clearly superior, as with handsaws. These saws cut on the pull stroke, rather than on the push stroke as do western saws; this means that the saw blade can be very thin. Thin blades leave a thinner kerf, or cut, and require less effort. Most woodworkers also find that they have better control

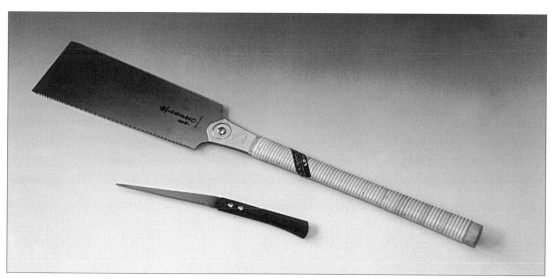

A Japanese handsaw, top, is ideal for this project. It cuts on the pull stroke and offers better control than western-style saws, which cut on the push stroke. The keyhole saw is also handy; this is a Japanese version developed for trimming bonsai trees.

when cutting on a pull stroke. Of the many types of Japanese saws available, the *ryoba noko giri* is most versatile. It has a flexible blade with crosscutting (cutting against the grain) teeth along one side and ripping (cutting with the grain) teeth along the other.

A small keyhole saw is optional, but useful. Again I recommend the Japanese version, particularly the type that looks like a steak knife but that was developed for trimming bonsai trees. These saws are inexpensive and can cut sharp curves, as required if you decide to fit watertight inspection ports on the bulkheads. The Japan Woodworker Company in Alameda, California, stocks a large selection of Japanese saws and other tools; its address is in appendix 2.

Although we could cut all the pieces with a handsaw, most of us will prefer to save time and use a power saw. A saber saw is the usual choice when cutting curved shapes, and it's important to choose one of top quality. Cheap saber saws vibrate and wander, leaving a mangled cut that looks chewed by a rodent. Professional-quality saws are smooth, heavy, and support the blade so it doesn't wander. Bosch and Porter Cable saber saws have the best reputation among my boatbuilding friends.

In addition to, or instead of, a saber saw, a small circular saw is nice to have. My favorite is the 4½-inch Porter Cable worm-drive trim saw. It does a fine job of cutting gentle curves in plywood, so it's ideal for cutting the strakes on boats. It makes much smoother cuts than a saber saw and with a ripping guide attached, it'll even do a passable job of ripping solid wood for inwales and outwales. I've tried several small battery-powered circular saws, which resemble the plug-in Porter Cable, but the models are neither as smooth-cutting nor as powerful as the original.

A saber saw makes fast work of cutting planks. This Bosch model, left, is favored by many boatbuilders. The small Porter Cable circular saw, right, is another favorite for cutting planks.

ABOVE: *The Lie-Nielsen rabbet plane, left, and the Stanley model 90 bullnose plane, top right, are good choices for cutting rabbets. The smaller bullnose plane below will do a fine job of cutting rabbets but is too small to cut scarfs.* RIGHT: *A collection of planes in Bill's shop. Even with all the modern power tools at our disposal, a plane is often the best tool.*

A canoe's inwales and outwales are long strips of solid wood that are best cut on a table saw. But don't buy a table saw just for this project. Many lumberyards, particularly the smaller old-fashioned sort, will cut these parts for a few dollars. You might also find friends or neighbors willing to let you use their table saw for a few minutes, but be sure you understand how to safely operate this very dangerous tool. It's also possible to cut these parts with a circular saw or even a handsaw—after all, canoes were built before the advent of power tools.

Planes

Of all the tools in Bill's shop none is used as often as his favorite plane. Whether fit-

ting a small part, cutting a scarf joint, rounding an edge, fairing or smoothing a plank, or shaping a bulkhead, the plane sees duty. The most common type of plane used in boatbuilding is the block plane, but if you don't own a router, you'll need a more specialized type called a rabbet plane.

When you are building these boats,

If you plan to use a router to cut rabbets, then use this low-angle block plane for all other jobs.

a groove, or *rabbet*, must be cut at the bottom edge of each plank. The rabbets are admittedly easier to cut with an electric router. But if you prefer to cut them with a hand tool, you'll use a rabbet plane. A rabbet plane is simply a plane that cuts flush on one or both sides. This specialized plane can also be used like an ordinary plane for other tasks.

The Stanley model 90 bullnose plane is the best of the commonly available rabbet planes; it's solid and easy to adjust. The Stanley model 75 is a smaller and much less expensive version, but if this were your only plane, I'd invest in the model 90. On the other hand, if you already own a block plane or plan to buy one, the model 75 is fine. The Record model 778 rabbet plane and the almost identical Stanley 78 are more versatile, complex, and expensive; both models include a fence, which is handy. If woodworking is a serious hobby, check them out.

A plane is also used for cutting scarfs to join lengths of wood and to smooth, or *fair*, planks, as well as for numerous smaller jobs. If you plan to cut the rab-

bets with a router instead of a plane, then skip the rabbet plane and buy a block plane. Block planes are available in standard models, with an angle of about 20 degrees between the blade and the work surface, and in low-angle models, with an angle of 12½ degrees. The low-angle type is better suited to the cross-grain planing often required in boatbuilding. The models commonly found in boat shops are the Stanley model 60½ low-angle plane and the similar, but slightly nicer, Record 60½. If you already own a standard block plane or small bench plane, there's no need to buy a low-angle type. Almost any small plane can be used to cut scarfs and fair planks so long as it's sharp.

Of course, the ultimate boatbuilder's plane would combine a low-angle block plane with a rabbet plane. Lie-Nielsen of Maine makes just such a tool: the #140 low-angle skew block plane. Like all Lie-Nielsen tools, it is superbly crafted, frighteningly expensive, and an absolute joy to use. These tools are not for the casual woodworker; if this is how you'd describe yourself, don't waste your money. If, however, you're serious about boatbuilding and appreciate fine tools, you owe it to yourself to try one. But be warned: you'll probably find your wallet considerably lighter soon after, as I did.

No matter which sort of plane you use, it must be sharp and properly adjusted. In almost every boatbuilding class I teach, a student or two will sheepishly approach me to explain that they've "never been very good with a hand plane." Usually the tools they are holding look like they've been buried in the backyard for a few years. After I clean off the rust and sharpen and adjust their planes, they are delighted with their newfound skill. With the exception of those from Lie-Nielsen, planes are not properly sharpened at the factory these days. Buy a sharpening stone and learn to use it. Instructions for sharpening a plane's iron can be found in appendix 3.

As power tools increasingly dominate woodworking, more specialized hand tools such as rabbet planes are becoming difficult to find. Fortunately, several of the tool companies listed in appendix 2 stock such tools.

By the way, after your enlightening experience with Japanese saws, you may be tempted to buy a Japanese-style plane. These planes require considerable skill to prepare, sharpen, and use. I would not recommend them unless you're willing to devote a lot of time and effort to mastering them.

Drills

Although this tool will see a lot of use, you can get by with almost any drill; even the old-fashioned eggbeater type will make the $\frac{1}{16}$-inch holes required to connect the planks. In fact, a drill is one tool on which it's easy to save some money. Most woodworkers have switched to the rechargeable drills that are so heavily advertised by tool companies. I'll admit that I use one, and it is convenient to be free of a power cord. But plug-in drills are lighter, more powerful, and much less expensive than the rechargeable models. Is that power cord really such a big drawback? And why do you suppose they have to advertise the battery models?

You'll need a set of bits for your drill. Cheap drill bits bend and break. Get a small but high-quality set of brad-point bits and a couple of extra $\frac{1}{16}$-inch bits.

Tools for Measuring

Accurate measuring is critical to boatbuilding. You'll transfer dozens of measurements from the plans to wood, redrawing, or *laying out*, virtually every part of the canoe. If your parts are measured accurately, they will be easy to assemble and will form a smooth, fair hull. Inaccurately measured pieces will require endless fiddling and may result in a lumpy canoe.

One tool you'll use constantly is a tape measure; Stanley, Starrett Tools, and Lufkin make the best ones. The most durable and easiest to use are the 25-foot-long models with 1-inch-wide blades. A 12- or 18-inch metal rule divided into $\frac{1}{64}$-inch marks is handy for measuring critical thickness like scarf lines, fastener lengths, drill-bit diameters, and other small dimensions.

In addition to tools for measuring

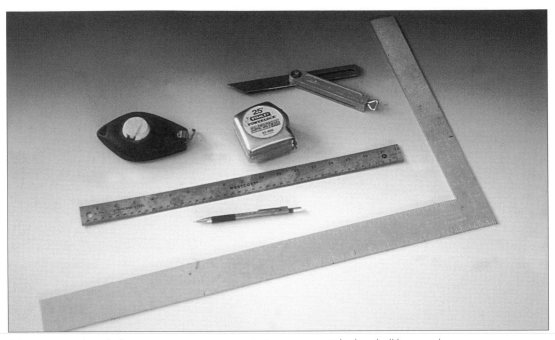

Measuring tools include a tape measure, carpenter's square, metal rule, chalkline, and pencil. You'll find use for a bevel gauge, too.

distances, you'll need a carpenter's square to ensure right angles when laying out the canoe's planks. The large 24- by 18-inch version is best. For laying out longer lines, you'll need a piece of thin string or a carpenter's chalkline. You'll also need a protractor or bevel gauge to measure angles. The bevel gauge is a traditional, and very useful, boatbuilder's tool; I think you'll find many chores for it after your canoe is launched.

A *batten* is simply a long, thin strip of wood that bends in a fair curve. It's used to draw the curves that define a boat's planks after the measurements from a set of plans have been transferred onto the plywood; think of it as flexible straightedge. Find or make a ¾- by ¾-inch piece of flexible wood with straight grain and no knots, splits, or other imperfections. It should be

at least 10 feet long, but longer is better. Battens last a lifetime, so it's well worth searching the lumberyard for a nice piece of wood from which to rip a collection of battens varying in thickness and stiffness. I know several builders who use window molding from a home-improvement store as batten stock. At Chesapeake Light Craft we often used a metal batten, which is nothing more than a 20-foot piece of square-section steel from the local welding shop. These steel battens are inexpensive and make perfect curves.

Once you've made a measurement, you'll need to mark it. Some woodworkers use only a knife or a scribe to make the mark because it leaves thinner lines than a pencil does. Actually, I prefer to use a sharp pencil because the line is easier to see. A draftsman's mechanical pencil is

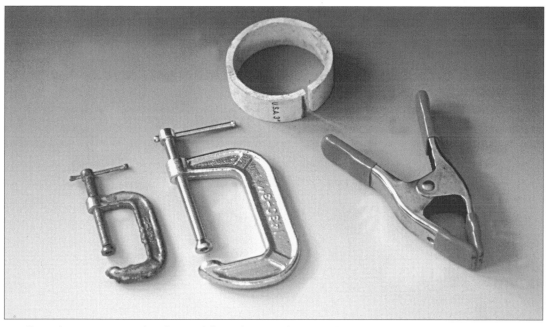

You'll need an assortment of C-clamps, left, and spring clamps, right. The round clamp is made from schedule-40 plastic drainpipe and is very effective.

best because it never needs sharpening, but I'm always losing mine. A useful, though not essential, tool is a marking gauge that's used to mark the position of the wire holes before stitching the planks together. Finally, an engineer's scale, architect's scale, and a calculator might come in handy when working from plans.

Before you start building, check all your measuring tools against one another. It's not uncommon to find that a tape doesn't agree exactly with a carpenter's square or rule. Usually the culprit is a bent tip on the end of the tape.

Clamps

A boatbuilder's tools always include a huge assortment of clamps; many boat shops have hundreds. I wouldn't start any project without a dozen C-clamps and a few spring clamps that can be operated with one hand.

When you are building the Sassafras canoes, the operation that requires the most clamps is installing the gunwales. Although it is possible to use screws instead of clamps to install the gunwales, clamps make the job a lot easier and faster. You'll need a clamp every 6 to 12 inches along the gunwales. So a 14-foot canoe will require 14 to 28 clamps, or 28 to 56 clamps if you plan to glue on both gunwales at once. Most of these should be C-clamps 2 inches or larger. By the way, the price of C-clamps varies greatly: I've seen identical 2-inch C-clamps priced from $1.39 to $3.69, so shop around.

You can also make your own clamps for a few cents each from schedule-40

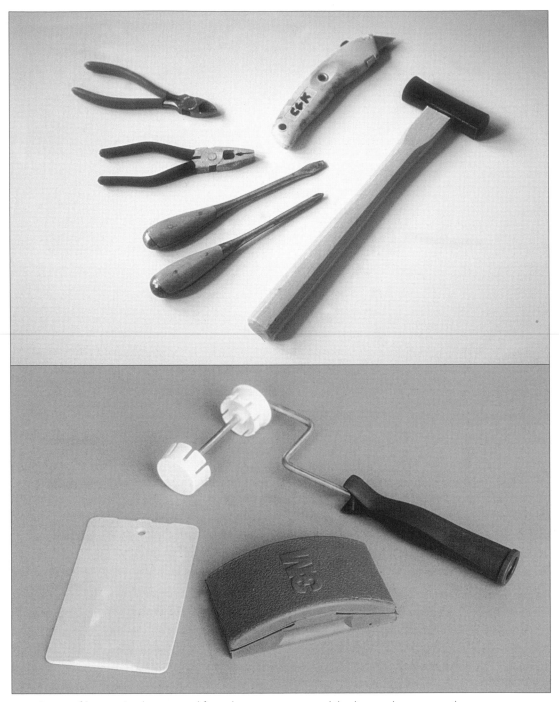

TOP: *A pair of lineman's pliers is used for tightening tie wires, while diagonal cutters are the best tools for removing them. Other miscellaneous tools include screwdrivers, a razor knife, and a small hammer.* **BOTTOM:** *A small rubber sanding block, an epoxy spreader, or squeegee, and a short roller frame are among the supplies you'll want for any boatbuilding project.*

plastic drainpipe. Cut a length of 4-inch-diameter pipe into 1½-inch rings (don't use your new Japanese saw for this). Split each ring, and you'll have spring clamps with enough clamping pressure for most epoxy joints. If more pressure is required, make the rings wider. These are not as convenient to use as C-clamps, but they will do the job.

Miscellaneous Hand Tools

For any boatbuilding project, you'll need an assortment of small tools, most of which are probably in your toolbox. Twisting all the wires that temporarily hold the planks together requires a pair of pliers; most any sort will do, but lineman's pliers or mechanic's pliers with large jaws are best. Later, wire cutters are needed to remove all those wires. The diagonal type, sometimes called side-cutters, is most efficient. You'll also need a couple of screwdrivers—Phillips and flathead—and a razor knife.

Even if you have an electric sander, you'll need a sanding block. The only type to get is the flexible solid rubber sort that takes a quarter-width strip of sandpaper. 3M makes these, but less expensive imitations are available. Finally, a coarse file or rasp will make short work of cleaning up epoxy drips and smoothing the overlapping plank edge.

Safety Gear

Don't skimp on eye protection, ear protectors, dust masks, and a respirator; they protect your most valuable tools.

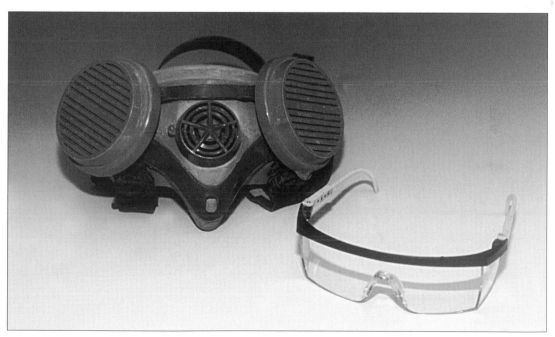

Don't forget a respirator and safety glasses.

A puff of sawdust in the eye when cutting has ruined more that one plank; a flying splinter could leave you blind. I prefer eye protectors that resemble eyeglasses. I fit them with neoprene eyeglass retainers so they always hang around my neck when I'm in the shop. It's worth paying a little more for eye protectors that don't distort your vision and don't scratch easily.

I consider it essential to use earplugs or hearing protectors when using a router or power saw. There is no question that my hearing suffers from not having used them when I was younger. The disposable, inexpensive foam earplugs work well but are troublesome to insert. Reusable earplugs that are attached to a short cord that hangs around your neck are better. But I like the ear protectors that resemble stereo headphones best, primarily because they are no trouble to put on and take off.

A dust mask is good idea when sanding. One boatbuilder I know eventually became allergic to sawdust and had to close his shop. The 3M paper masks with the little aluminum piece to bend around your nose are favored by many boatbuilders. Of course, paper masks only stop dust; to protect your lungs from paint and other fumes, a respirator is required. There are many styles and types of respirators, and it's well worth asking for advice at a professional paint supplier or industrial supply house before choosing a model. Some of the new models are very light and quite comfortable.

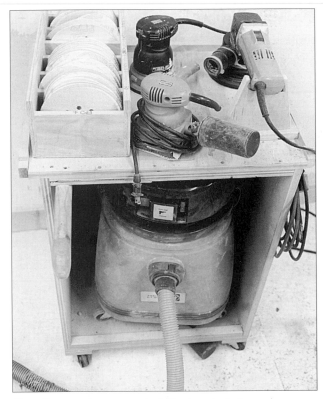

The rolling sanding station in Bill's shop includes a shop vacuum that can be connected to any of his sanders. This is effective in keeping the work area sawdust free.

Sanders

Although you could sand your canoe by hand, you would need close to a full day to do a proper job, and the boat will need to be sanded at least twice during construction. So most of us will choose to invest in a small electric sander.

Random-orbital sanders eliminate much of the tedium of this task. They do the job quickly and don't leave swirl marks. The better models have effective dust-removal systems, and hook-and-loop pads make quick work of changing paper. I'm most impressed with the 5-inch Bosch and Porter Cable sanders.

If you don't mind a slightly slower machine, one of the best inexpensive sanders is the quarter-sheet Makita palm

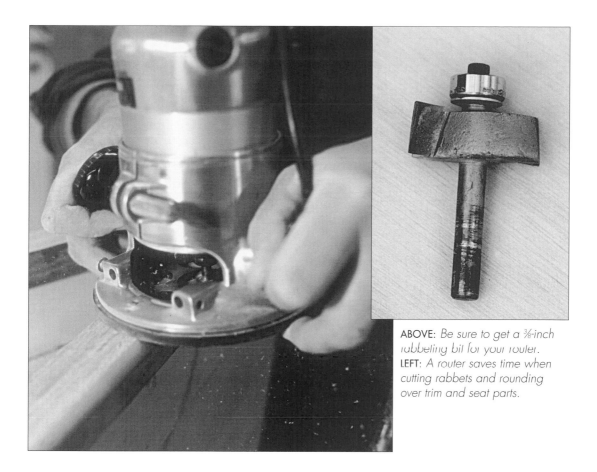

ABOVE: *Be sure to get a ⅜-inch rabbeting bit for your router.*
LEFT: *A router saves time when cutting rabbets and rounding over trim and seat parts.*

sander. It sands fast enough so that you'll see progress, but not so fast that you'll accidentally sand through layers of plywood or fiberglass. Quarter-sheet sanders use inexpensive sheet sandpaper rather than costly hook-and-loop pads. Several companies make similar models, but the Makita fits my hand just so. Of course, it's possible that my hand has grown to fit the sander after all these years.

If your sander has a dust-pickup bag, consider removing the bag and connecting the sander to a shop vacuum cleaner. A simple adapter can be fashioned from some flexible plastic hose and a few hose clamps. You might also need a step-up adapter to join two sizes of hose. Dig around in the plumbing section of a home-improvement store to find the parts. Your shop will stay a lot cleaner for the effort.

Routers

Although it's not essential for this project, a router is one of the most versatile tools in your shop, and it'll save you a lot of time and effort in this project. You'll use a router to cut the rabbets in the strakes and to round over the inwales, outwales, thwart, and seat parts. I recommend a simple, but heavy-duty, router between ¾ and 2 horsepower. The no-nonsense Porter Cable 1½-horsepower router seems almost indestructible and is a favorite of many boatbuilders. Stay away from plunge routers and models loaded with extra features unless you have a specific future need for them. A router is little more than a smooth and powerful high-rpm motor and an adjustable base, and that's what you should be paying for.

You'll need a few bits for your router. For this project, get a ⅜-inch rabbeting bit, the sort with a bearing at the bottom. A ¼-inch round-over bit is also handy for finishing gunwales, thwarts, and seats. There are many good brands of router bits; I've been satisfied with Amana, Freud, and CMT bits, among others.

Supplies

In addition to tools, you'll need the following supplies; many of these items are discussed in more detail in the construction chapters.

- Sandpaper—80-, 220-, and 400-grit
- Disposable foam brushes with wooden, not plastic, handles
- Disposable bristle brushes, also called chip brushes
- Disposable foam rollers. These must be the short-nap yellow rollers that are also used for applying epoxy or lacquer.
- Epoxy syringes, small size (most epoxy companies sell these)

- Plastic epoxy spreader or squeegees (plastic auto-body spreaders from the auto-parts store will do)
- Plastic sheet (piece of a painter's tarp) or wax paper
- Epoxy-metering pumps or measuring cups (these may be included when you buy an epoxy kit)
- Stirring sticks (use Popsicle sticks, or make your own)
- Masking tape (3M Fine Line tape is by far the best)
- 1-inch brads
- Disposable gloves (it's economical to buy a box of 100)

Setting Up Shop

You don't need a real woodworking shop to build a canoe; a garage, a porch, a basement storeroom, or even the backyard can be your shop. It need be only a few feet longer and wider than the boat you're building and equipped with a table or workbench and a pair of sawhorses. When gluing the planks, you'll need a flat surface as long as the canoe, but this can be a hallway or garage floor.

Good light and ventilation are also essential. You'll need to see well to judge curves, joints, and the surface quality of wood. And you must be certain that the almost colorless epoxy is evenly and completely spread over surfaces to be joined. If your shop isn't well lit, buy an inexpensive 48-inch fluorescent light fixture and hang it from the rafters or ceiling.

Building these canoes involves work-

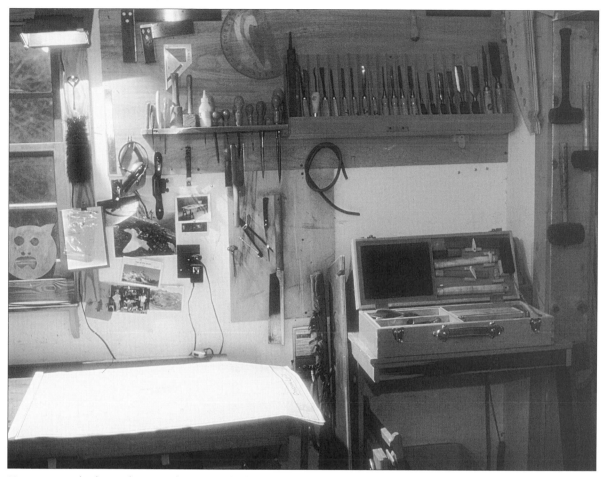

Keep your tools clean, sharp, and organized. This is the area next to one of Bill's workbenches.

ing with epoxy resins, hardeners, varnish, and paint, and it produces copious quantities of sawdust. Breathing in these fumes and particles is both unhealthy and unpleasant. Your shop must have enough doors or windows for good ventilation. If it doesn't, or if you're building during winter, install an exhaust fan. This can simply be a household fan set on a windowsill. In either case, use your respirator.

If you plan to use power tools, remember that they draw considerable amperage. If your shop's electrical power is supplied by an extension cord, be sure it's rated for the job. Any extension cord used with power tools should be of at least 14-gauge wire (12-gauge is better); the longer the cord, the more crucial heavy wire is. Your tools will still operate if you use a thin cord, but they'll overheat and might burn out.

Epoxy should be used within the temperature range specified be the manufacturer, usually between 60°F and 80°F.

During winter or on cold nights, your shop should be heated. My first shop was a small, uninsulated garage warmed by two portable electric heaters. They provided sufficient warmth on all but the coldest nights. On very cold nights, you can make a heated "tent" by draping a plastic tarp over your canoe and aiming a heater under it. Just don't let the heater touch the plastic, or fires may impede your progress.

CHAPTER FOUR

▶*The Plans*

The elements of canoe design have been understood for over a hundred years, so any boat designer can draw a satisfactory hull. Yet there are hundreds of models of canoes on the market, each one slightly different. Even if we put aside differences in construction methods and materials, we find a staggering variety of hull shapes. Most are quite similar, yet no two are identical, and experienced paddlers obsess over these minor differences. This hull has a bit more rocker, that one is a little broader at the waterline; one hull has flare, the other, tumblehome.

For many of us, a small boat is our little slice of perfection. Our houses always need some minor repair, we may never find the perfect car, there's no point in talking about a perfect job, but a small boat should be exactly what we want. And it can take us away from the rest. So these plans are my interpretation of the perfect canoe. Of course, we must be realistic in our expectations. We can't expect a boat to both maneuver in whitewater and track straight across a wide, lumpy lake. And a canoe that's fun to paddle solo won't hold a family of four and all its gear. The art of boat design is, like so many things, the art of compromise.

Reading the Plans

Although draftsmen and designers really do strive to draw plans that are easy to understand, deciphering boat plans can be frustrating for novice and experienced builders alike. I spent too many youthful years sitting in my office at a civil-engineering firm answering questions from contractors, developers, and county inspectors who couldn't understand something in our plans. I spent the next eight years at my own company; again, much of that time was given to answering questions about plans—at least these were plans for boats rather than shopping centers. It was still frustrating; my plans, which seemed so simple to me, confused builders who had a slightly different way of thinking. Sometimes we simply don't "get" what the designer intends; it helps to take a break, put the plans aside, and look at them again in the morning.

I hope you'll find the plans in this book easy to understand. They are complete and contain all the information required to build the Sassafras canoes. Should you choose to build from the plans offered here, you'll need to scale up some patterns and redraw most of the parts to full size, but that's really not too difficult. Exact dimensions are given for all the strakes, critical hull parts, and bulkheads.

But if you'd like full-size plans, they are available from Chesapeake Light Craft at the address in appendix 2. There are several good reasons to buy a full-size set. Plan purchase entitles you to telephone or E-mail technical support. The plans will contain the latest revisions; builders often call with new ideas and to point out errors on plans. Small parts will be drawn full size, so you need only to trace them rather than scale them up.

The Sassafras canoe plans are very simple compared with most boat plans. On the first sheet is a *profile* view showing the boat from the side; a *half-breadth*, or *plan*, view showing the boat from the top; and a *body plan*, showing a combination front-and-back view. A set of lines resembling and serving the same purpose as contour lines on a map is superimposed over the profile view and the body plan. These drawings are called the boat's lines. An experienced boatbuilder can learn much about the shape of the hull from these lines and could in fact measure and scale them to full size using a process called *lofting*, possibly even building the boat with no other information. If this is your first boatbuilding project, the lines may seem confusing, but it's important to study them so you can imagine how the boat's hull should look.

Also on the first sheet is a cutaway profile view identifying various parts and showing the locations of the seats, thwart, and bulkheads. You've probably noticed some lines on the plan view pointing to the letters A, B, and C. These mark the locations of the cross-section views on the left side of the plan sheet. Cross section A-A, for example, is along the line connecting those two letters. Because the letters are to the left of the cross-section line, it indicates that the view is looking to the left or toward the bow. Other information on the first sheet includes the boat's dimensions and some miscellaneous notes on building.

The plans also contain a drawing showing the alignment of the planks and various construction details. Sheet 3 shows more construction details and patterns for the decks and bulkheads and other parts. The last sheet of the plans is devoted to the shape of the planks. In the next chapter, we will use this sheet to cut all the planks for our canoe. Don't worry; it's not as complicated as it looks.

Some builders may wonder why I don't provide full-size patterns for hull panels. I've learned never to use these. Modern printing methods are simply not accurate enough to produce inexpensive scale drawings in the 8-foot-long sheets required. By the time the end of the sheet of paper has passed through the printer's rollers, the drawing could be distorted by several inches. When Chesapeake Light Craft published full-size patterns for my designs, it was rewarded with phone calls from angry builders claiming that their panels didn't fit well. Experienced builders said that it was far more time-consuming to crawl around on the floor tracing 16-foot panels than to simply lay them out using scale plans.

Sassafras 12

Imagine a boat so light that you can put it on your shoulder and stroll casually down a wooded trail, carry it to a hidden lake or stream, or paddle it with almost no effort. That was the idea behind the original ultralight "trapper" or "pack" canoes: they could be carried into roadless areas for hunting or fishing. The 26-pound Sassafras 12 carries on the tradition, but with modern building methods.

If you stop and think about how most canoes are used, or how we'd like to use them, a small ultralight like this boat makes surprisingly good sense. Most of us don't get out on the water as often as we'd wish because it's difficult to find a paddling partner on short notice, or we only have a few hours after work and it's too much trouble to load an 85-pound canoe, or we want to go fishing or birding on a small stream and a 16-foot canoe is simply too big. We need a tiny boat that we can grab with one hand, throw on top of the car, and be off in 10 minutes. Casual paddling, that's what this 12-footer is for.

Although the Sassafras 12 can be portaged and paddled by a child, it'll hold a 225-pound load. It tracks well, is easy to turn, and is stable enough for fishing. For maximum efficiency, you'll want to paddle the Sassafras 12 with a double (kayak) paddle, but traditionalists will find it also moves beautifully with a canoe paddle.

The 12-footer is built from 4 mm plywood (hardwood is used for gunwales and other trim) and is, by a small margin, the simplest and least expensive of these canoes to build. *(continued on page 44)*

The Sassafras 12 is perfect for a leisurely paddle on calm water.

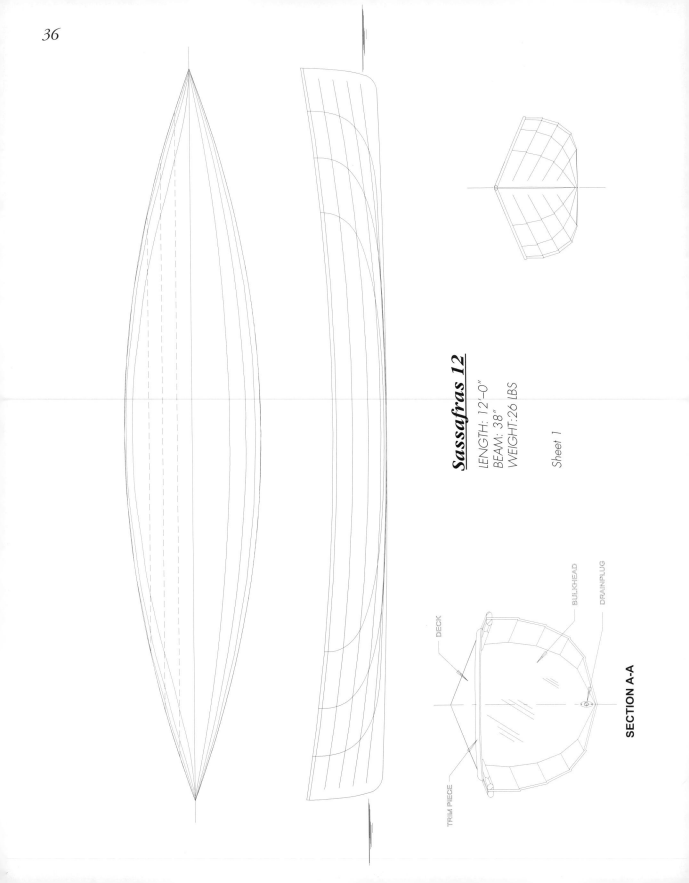

Sassafras 12

LENGTH: 12'-0"
BEAM: 38"
WEIGHT: 26 LBS

Sheet 1

DECK

BULKHEAD

DRAINPLUG

TRIM PIECE

SECTION A-A

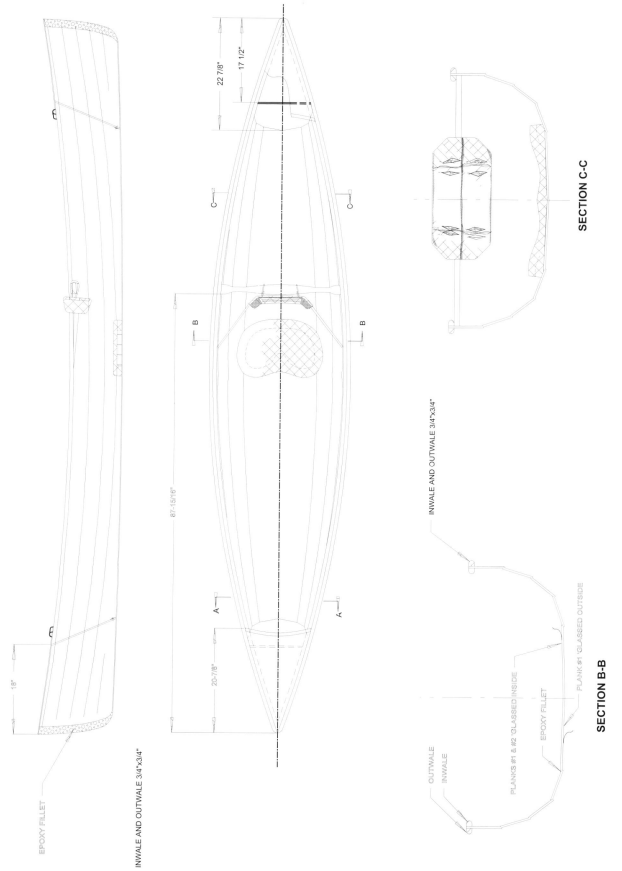

EPOXY FILLET

INWALE AND OUTWALE 3/4"×3/4"

18"

87-15/16"

20-7/8"

22 7/8"

17 1/2"

B

B

C

C

A

A

SECTION C-C

INWALE AND OUTWALE 3/4"×3/4"

OUTWALE

INWALE

PLANKS #1 & #2 'GLASSED INSIDE

EPOXY FILLET

PLANK #1 'GLASSED OUTSIDE

SECTION B-B

Sheet 1

38

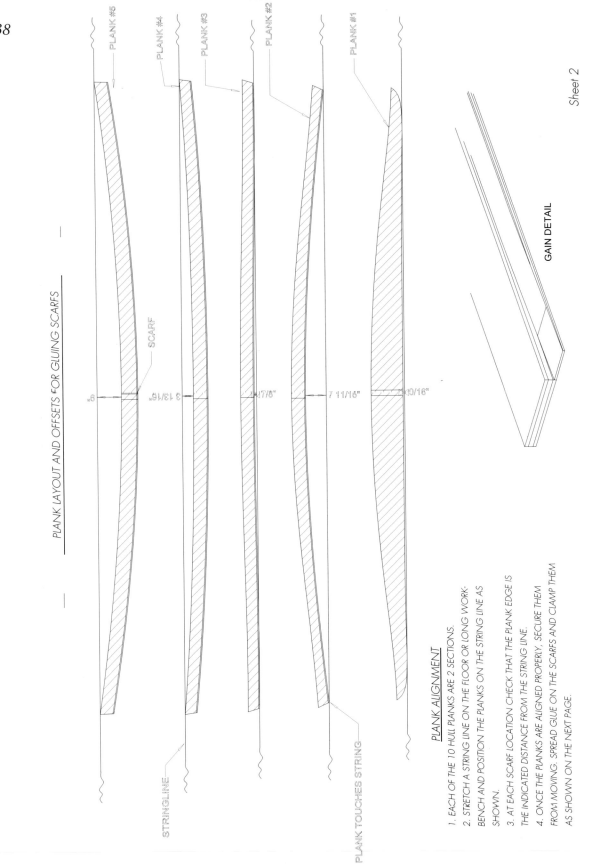

PLANK LAYOUT AND OFFSETS FOR GLUING SCARFS

PLANK #5
PLANK #4
PLANK #3
PLANK #2
PLANK #1

SCARF

STRINGLINE

PLANK TOUCHES STRING

GAIN DETAIL

Sheet 2

PLANK ALIGNMENT

1. EACH OF THE 10 HULL PLANKS ARE 2 SECTIONS.

2. STRETCH A STRING LINE ON THE FLOOR OR LONG WORK-
BENCH AND POSITION THE PLANKS ON THE STRING LINE AS
SHOWN.

3. AT EACH SCARF LOCATION CHECK THAT THE PLANK EDGE IS
THE INDICATED DISTANCE FROM THE STRING LINE.

4. ONCE THE PLANKS ARE ALIGNED PROPERLY, SECURE THEM
FROM MOVING. SPREAD GLUE ON THE SCARFS AND CLAMP THEM
AS SHOWN ON THE NEXT PAGE.

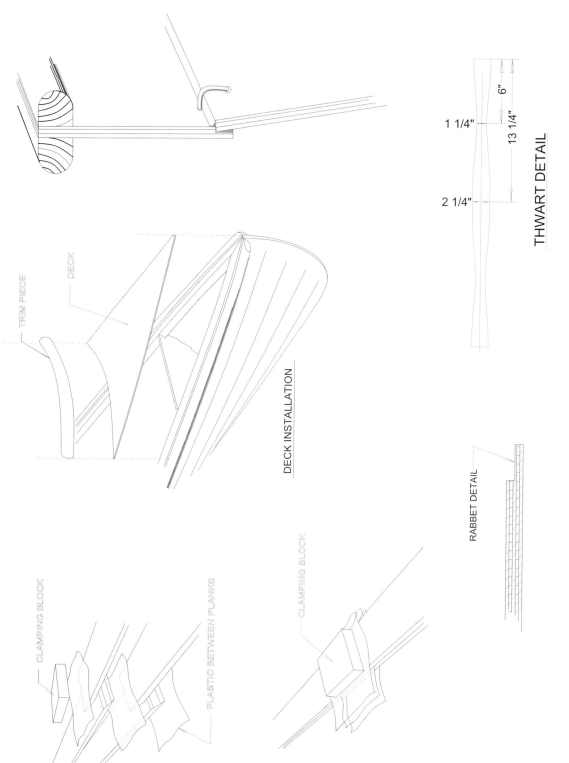

THWART DETAIL

6"

1 1/4"

13 1/4"

2 1/4"

TRIM PIECE

DECK

DECK INSTALLATION

RABBET DETAIL

CLAMPING BLOCK

PLASTIC BETWEEN PLANKS

CLAMPING BLOCK

SCARF LENGTH IS 1-1/4"

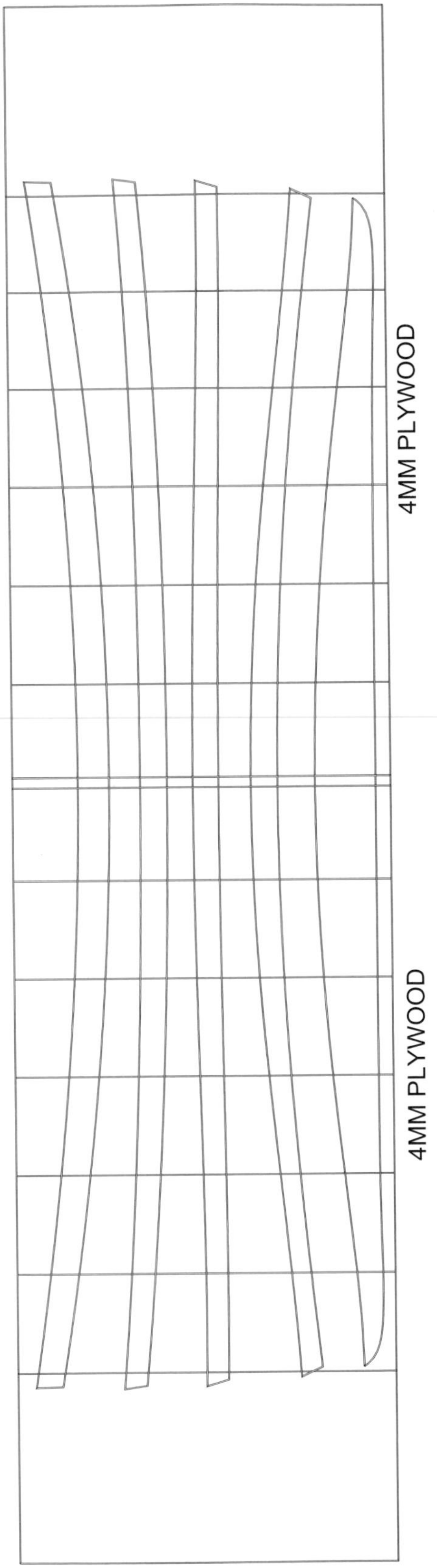

4MM PLYWOOD

4MM PLYWOOD

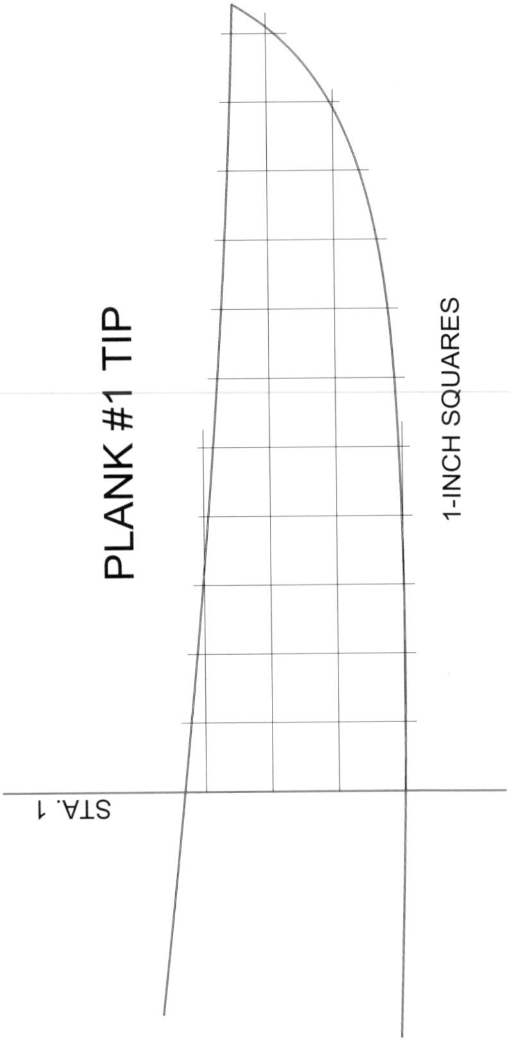

PLANK #1 TIP

STA. 1

1-INCH SQUARES

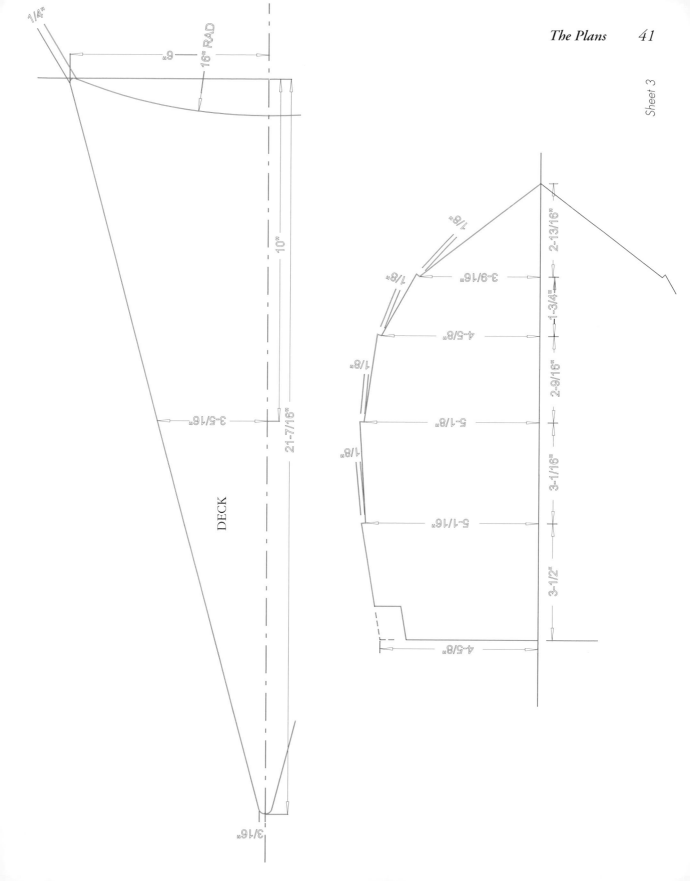

1/4"

6"

16" RAD

10"

3-5/16"

21-7/16"

DECK

3/16"

1/8"

1/8"

1/8"

1/8"

2-13/16"

1-3/4"

3-9/16"

4-5/8"

2-9/16"

5-1/8"

3-1/16"

5-1/16"

3-1/2"

4-5/8"

USE THIS EDGE AS BASELINE

96" X 48" X 4MM PLYWOOD

SEE FULL SIZE PATTERN

SASSAFRAS 12 PLANK LAYOUT *Sheet 4*

(continued from page 35)

SASSAFRAS 12 BILL OF MATERIALS

- 4 sheets 4 mm BS1088 okoume marine plywood
- 1 gallon marine-grade epoxy (total quantity of resin plus hardener)
- ½ gallon (by volume) wood-flour thickener for epoxy
- ½ gallon (by volume) silica thickener for epoxy
- 4 yards of 6-ounce, 50-inch-wide fiberglass cloth
- 150 feet of 18-gauge bare copper single-strand wire
- 4 pieces ¾-inch-square by 12-foot, 6-inch ash, mahogany, or other hardwood for inwales and outwales
- 28-inch canoe thwart or hardwood to make your own
- 4 #10 by 1¼-inch stainless steel wood screws or 2 stainless steel ¼- by 1¾-inch bolts, washers, and nuts for mounting thwart
- Hardwood to make deck trim pieces (see plan dimensions)
- Commercial kayak seat and mounting kit or ¾-inch closed-cell foam to make seat shown in chapter 9
- Whitewater-style kayak backband and mounting hardware

Sassafras 14

This 14-footer makes a fine solo canoe, but it's also big enough for two day-paddlers. It performs best when fitted with a single seat amidships. The solo paddler will find this boat holds enough gear for an extended camping trip and is reassuringly stable when crossing a windy lake. And that solo paddler who prefers to paddle from a kneeling position will also delight in the Sassafras 14's handling.

Fishermen will find room for lots of gear and a fair-size cooler. But the real beauty of this model is that you can take along a friend on occasion. This boat is a little tippy for two, be warned, but with a little practice, you'll feel comfortable in it.

The Sassafras 14 can be built from 4 mm plywood to save weight or 6 mm to increase strength. I prefer the 4 mm version, which is also easier to build because the planks are easier to bend into position.

SASSAFRAS 14 BILL OF MATERIALS

- 4 4- by 8-foot sheets 4 mm BS1088 okoume marine plywood
- 1½ gallons marine-grade epoxy (total quantity of resin plus hardener)
- ½ gallon (by volume) wood-flour thickener for epoxy
- ½ gallon (by volume) silica thickener for epoxy
- 5 yards of 6-ounce, 50-inch-wide fiberglass cloth
- 200 feet of 18-gauge bare copper single-strand wire
- 4 pieces ¾-inch-square by 16-foot ash, mahogany, or other hardwood for inwales and outwales
- 32-inch canoe thwart or hardwood to make your own

ABOVE: *Bill and Ansley Thomas try out the Sassafras 14.* RIGHT: *The Sassafras 14 is a fine choice for the skilled solo paddler.*

- 4 #10 by 1¼-inch stainless steel wood screws or 2 stainless steel ¼- by 1¾-inch bolts, washers, and nuts for mounting thwart

- Hardwood to make deck trim pieces and doublers for hanging seats (see plan dimensions)

- 2 commercial canoe seats or materials to make one of the seat types shown in chapter 9

- 2 commercial seat-hanging kits or spacers and bolts as described in chapter 9

(continued on page 62)

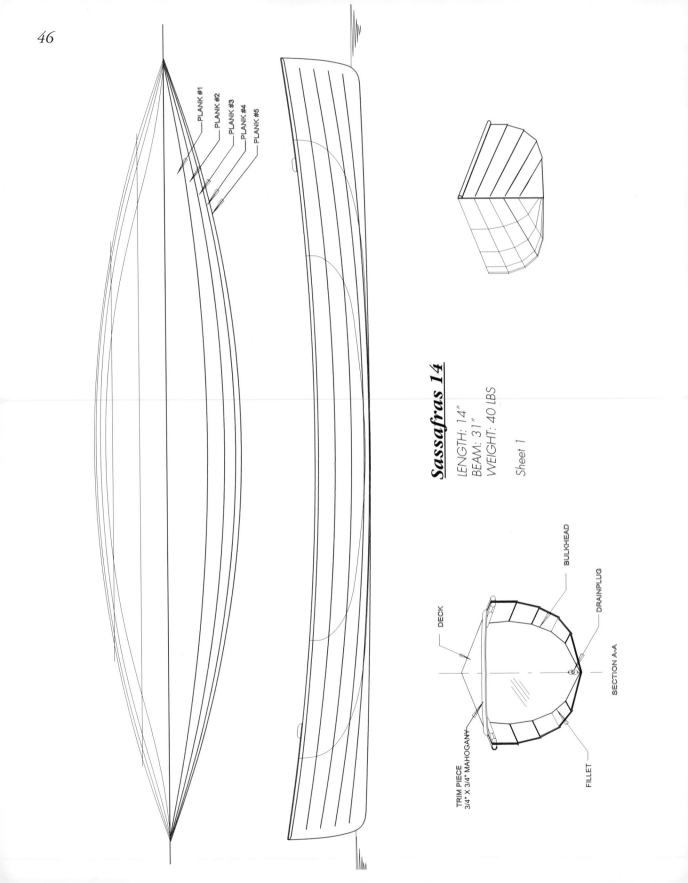

PLANK #1
PLANK #2
PLANK #3
PLANK #4
PLANK #5

Sassafras 14

LENGTH: 14"
BEAM: 31"
WEIGHT: 40 LBS

Sheet 1

DECK

BULKHEAD

DRAINPLUG

TRIM PIECE
3/4" X 3/4" MAHOGANY

FILLET

SECTION A-A

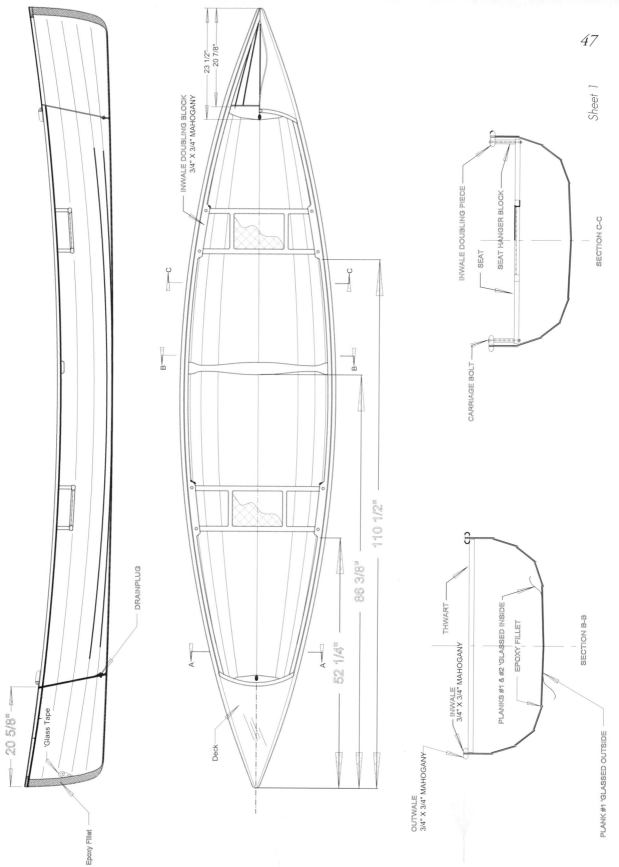

47

Sheet 1

20 5/8"

Epoxy Fillet

'Glass Tape

DRAINPLUG

INWALE DOUBLING BLOCK
3/4" X 3/4" MAHOGANY

23 1/2"
20 7/8"

C

C

B

B

A

A

110 1/2"

86 3/8"

52 1/4"

Deck

INWALE DOUBLING PIECE

SEAT

SEAT HANGER BLOCK

CARRIAGE BOLT

SECTION C-C

THWART

INWALE
3/4" X 3/4" MAHOGANY

PLANKS #1 & #2 'GLASSED INSIDE

EPOXY FILLET

SECTION B-B

OUTWALE
3/4" X 3/4" MAHOGANY

PLANK #1 'GLASSED OUTSIDE

PLANK LAYOUT AND OFFSETS FOR GLUING SCARFS

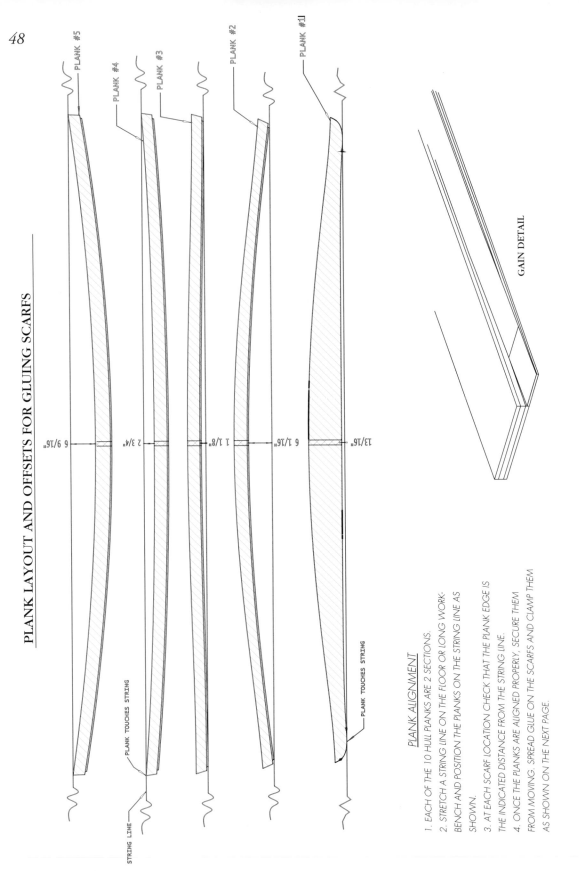

PLANK #5

PLANK #4

PLANK #3

PLANK #2

PLANK #1

6 9/16"

2 3/4"

1 1/8"

6 1/16"

13/16"

PLANK TOUCHES STRING

PLANK TOUCHES STRING

STRING LINE

GAIN DETAIL

Sheet 2

PLANK ALIGNMENT

1. EACH OF THE 10 HULL PLANKS ARE 2 SECTIONS.

2. STRETCH A STRING LINE ON THE FLOOR OR LONG WORK-
BENCH AND POSITION THE PLANKS ON THE STRING LINE AS
SHOWN.

3. AT EACH SCARF LOCATION CHECK THAT THE PLANK EDGE IS
THE INDICATED DISTANCE FROM THE STRING LINE.

4. ONCE THE PLANKS ARE ALIGNED PROPERLY, SECURE THEM
FROM MOVING. SPREAD GLUE ON THE SCARFS AND CLAMP THEM
AS SHOWN ON THE NEXT PAGE.

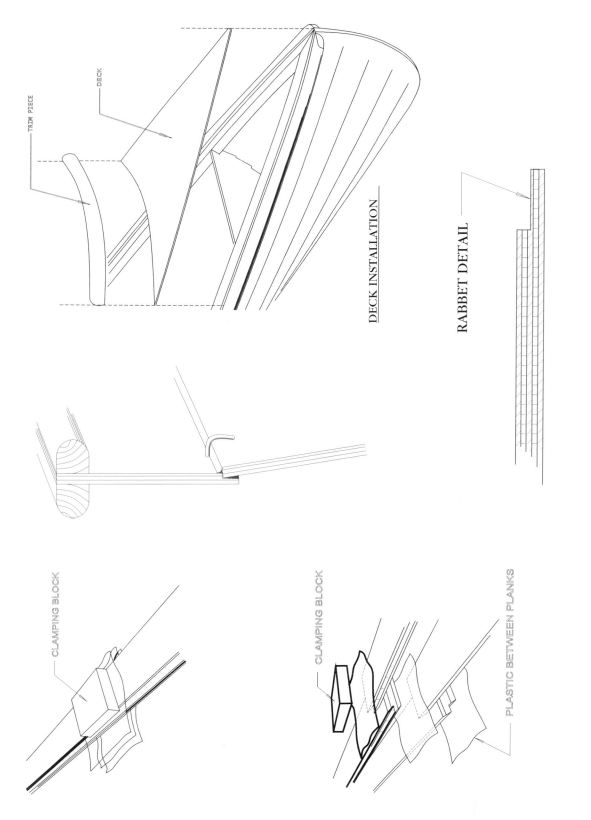

TRIM PIECE

DECK

DECK INSTALLATION

RABBET DETAIL

CLAMPING BLOCK

CLAMPING BLOCK

PLASTIC BETWEEN PLANKS

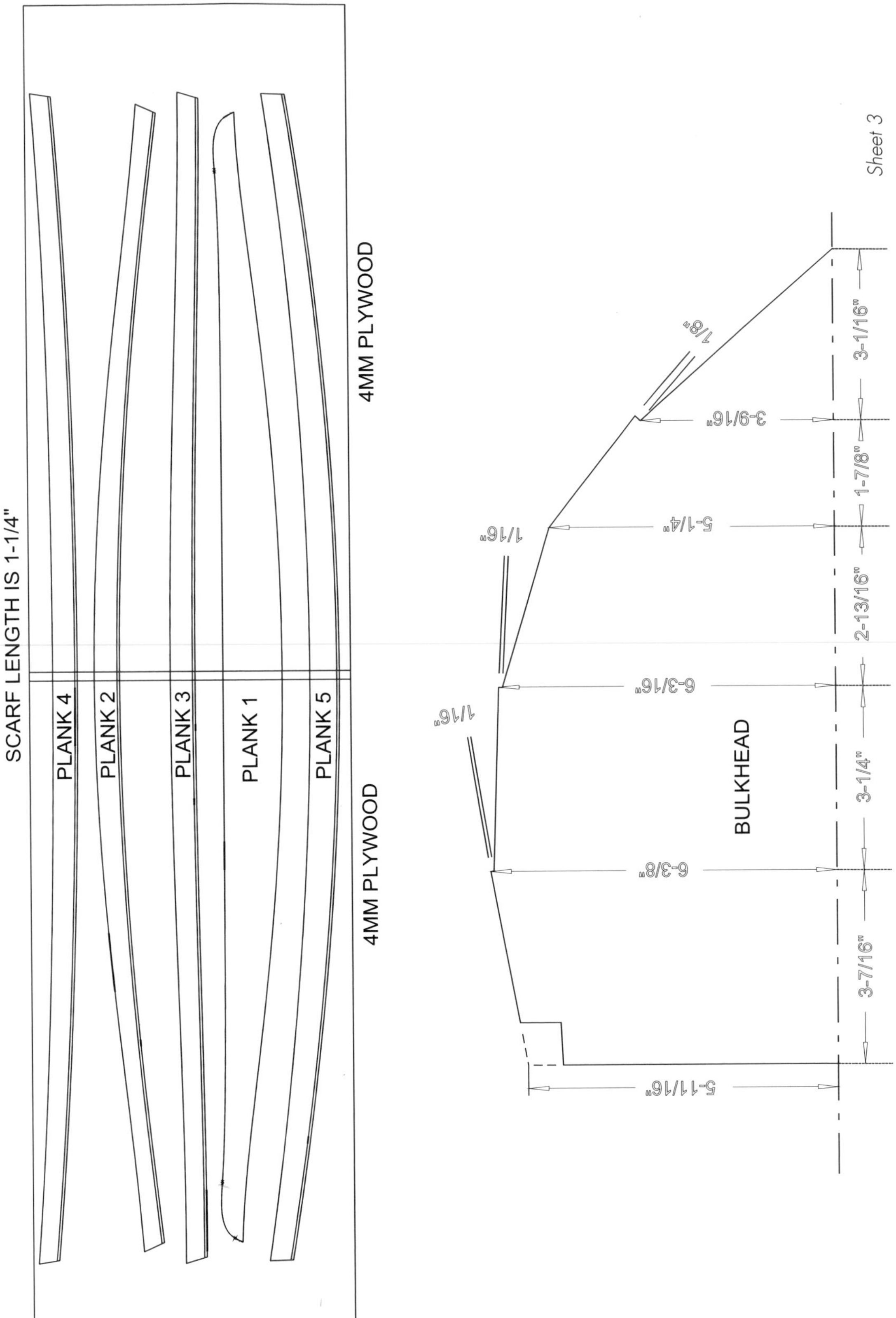

50

SCARF LENGTH IS 1-1/4"

4MM PLYWOOD

4MM PLYWOOD

PLANK 4

PLANK 2

PLANK 3

PLANK 1

PLANK 5

BULKHEAD

Sheet 3

3-1/16"

3-9/16"

1-7/8"

5-1/4"

2-13/16"

6-3/16"

3-1/4"

6-3/8"

3-7/16"

5-11/16"

1/8"

1/16"

1/16"

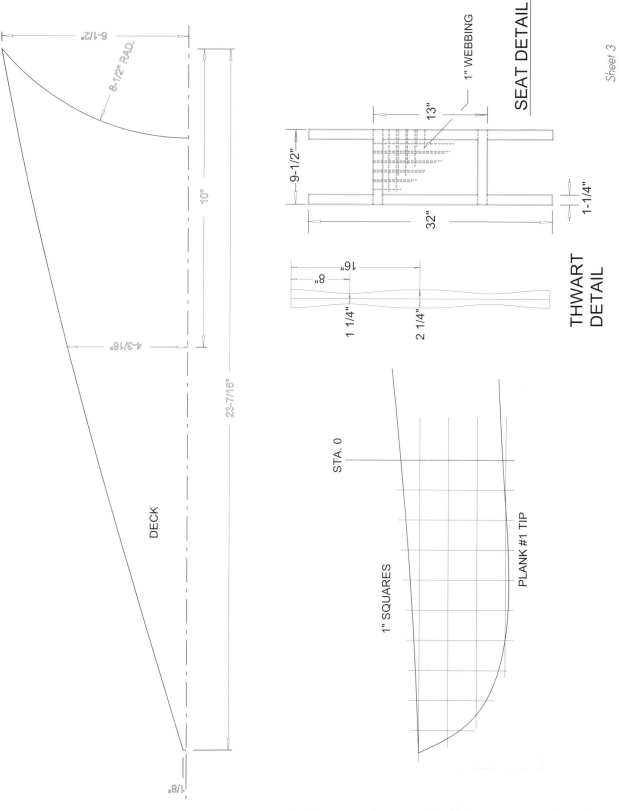

6-1/2"

8-1/2" RAD.

10"

4-3/16"

23-7/16"

DECK

1/8"

1" WEBBING

SEAT DETAIL

9-1/2"

13"

32"

1-1/4"

THWART DETAIL

16"

8"

1 1/4"

2 1/4"

STA. 0

1" SQUARES

PLANK #1 TIP

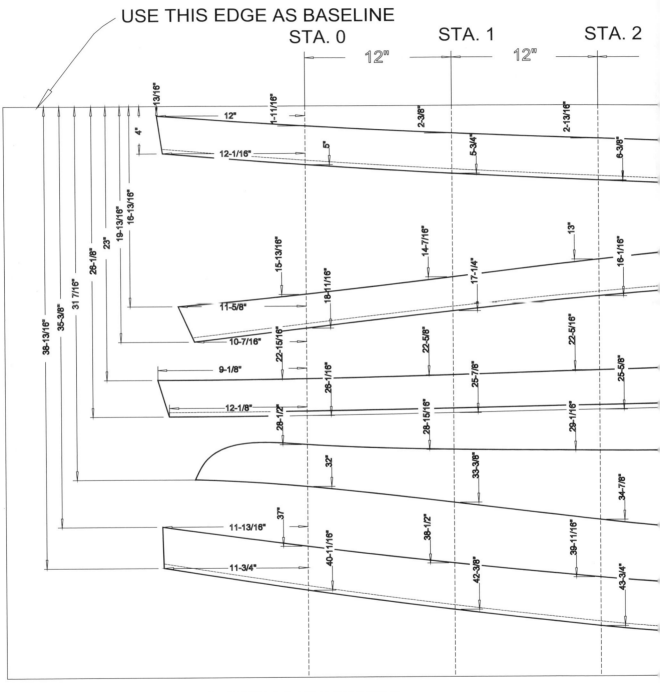

USE THIS EDGE AS BASELINE

SASSAFRAS 14 PLANK LAYOUT   Sheet 4

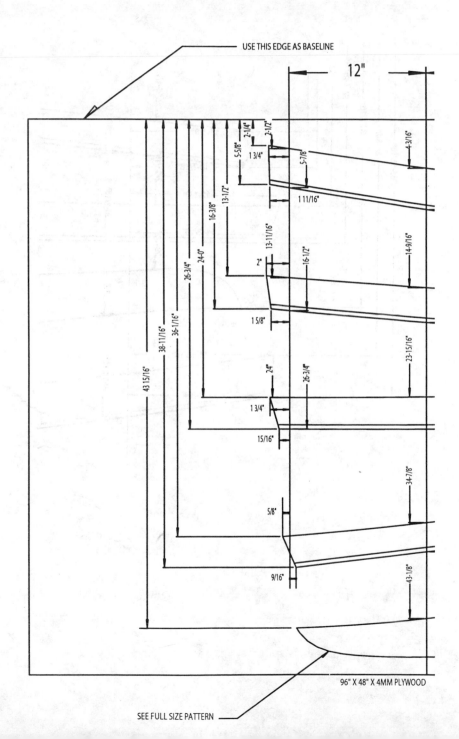

USE THIS EDGE AS BASELINE

12"

96" X 48" X 4MM PLYWOOD

SEE FULL SIZE PATTERN

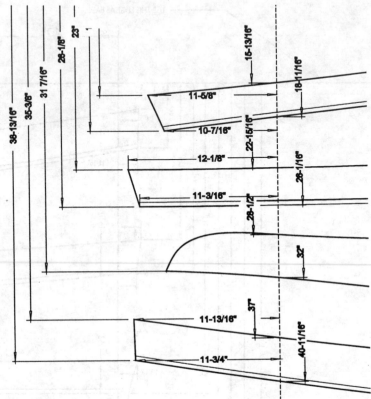

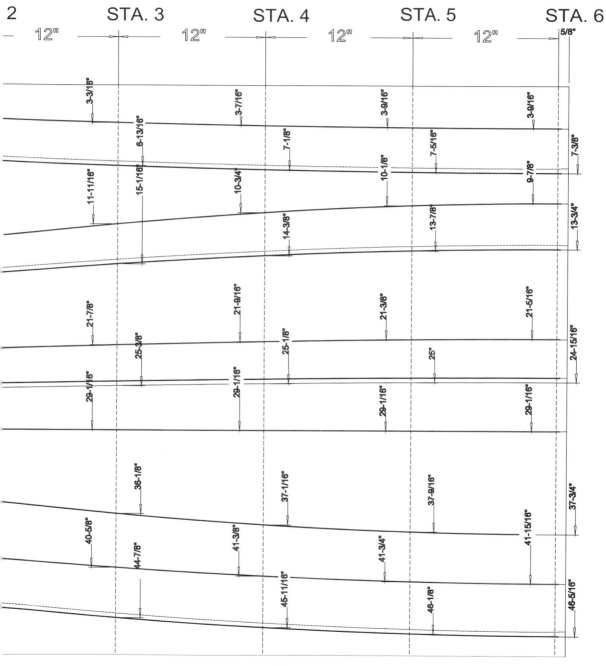

STA. 3   STA. 4   STA. 5   STA. 6

2

12"   12"   12"   12"   5/8"

3-3/16"   3-7/16"   3-9/16"   3-9/16"

6-13/16"   7-1/8"   7-5/16"   7-3/8"

15-1/16"   10-3/4"   10-1/8"   9-7/8"

11-11/16"   14-3/8"   13-7/8"   13-3/4"

21-7/8"   21-9/16"   21-3/8"   21-5/16"

25-3/8"   25-1/8"   25"   24-15/16"

29-1/16"   29-1/16"   29-1/16"   29-1/16"

36-1/8"   37-1/16"   37-9/16"   37-3/4"

40-5/8"   41-3/8"   41-3/4"   41-15/16"

44-7/8"   45-11/16"   46-1/8"   46-5/16"

4X8 4MM PLYWOOD

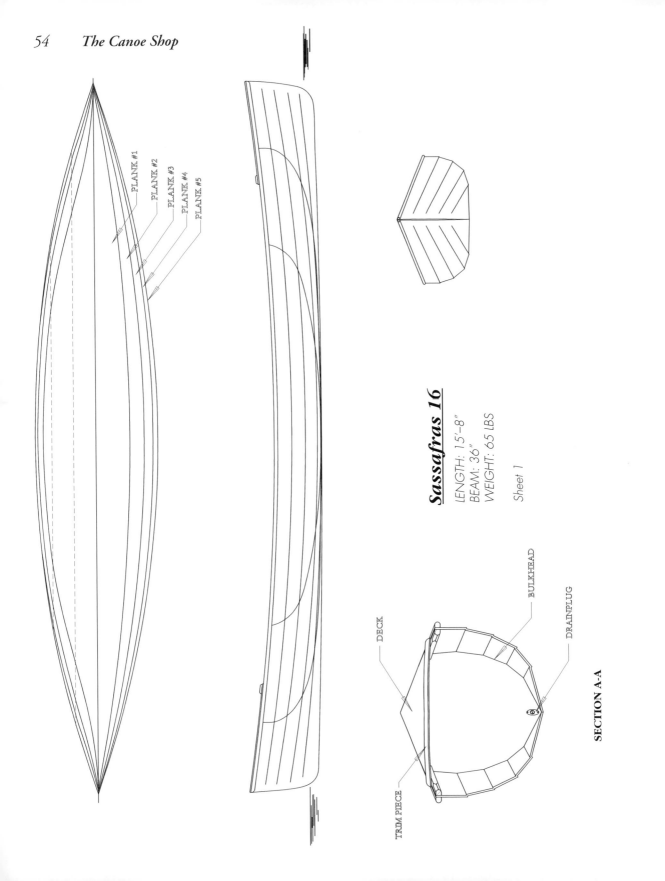

PLANK #1
PLANK #2
PLANK #3
PLANK #4
PLANK #5

Sassafras 16

LENGTH: 15'-8"
BEAM: 36"
WEIGHT: 65 LBS

Sheet 1

DECK

BULKHEAD

DRAINPLUG

TRIM PIECE

SECTION A-A

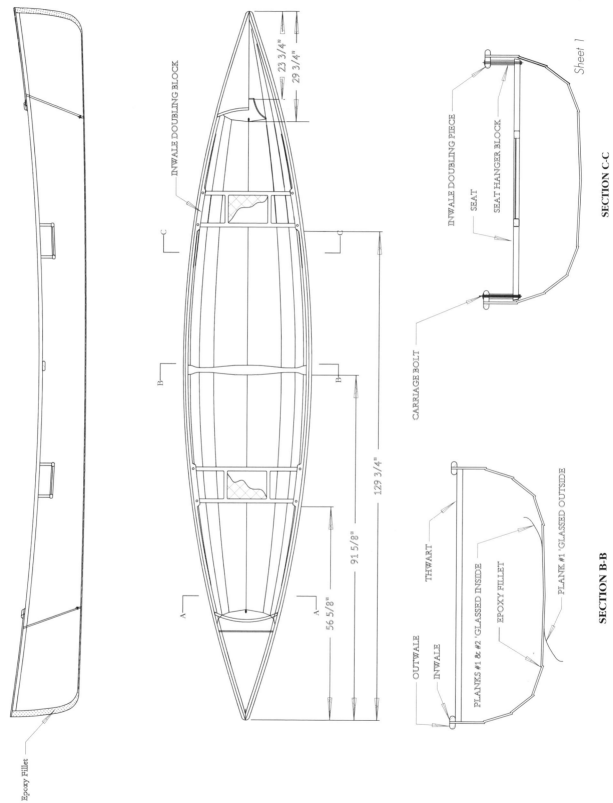

INWALE DOUBLING BLOCK

23 3/4"
29 3/4"

C

C

B

B

A

A

129 3/4"

91 5/8"

56 5/8"

Epoxy Fillet

SECTION C-C

Sheet 1

INWALE DOUBLING PIECE

SEAT

SEAT HANGER BLOCK

CARRIAGE BOLT

SECTION B-B

THWART

PLANK #2 'GLASSED INSIDE

EPOXY FILLET

PLANK #1 'GLASSED OUTSIDE

OUTWALE

INWALE

PLANKS #1 & #2 'GLASSED INSIDE

PLANK LAYOUT AND OFFSETS FOR GLUING SCARFS

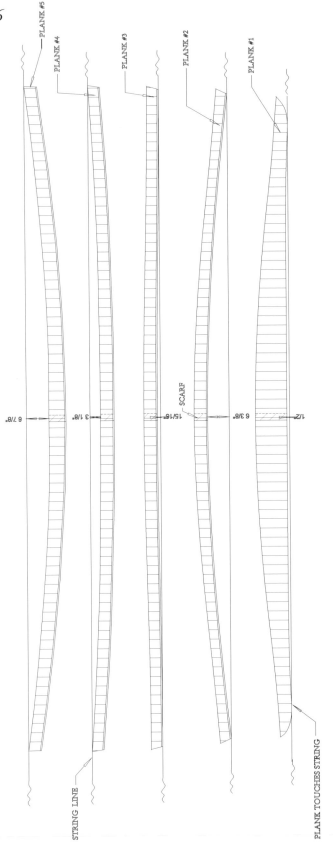

PLANK #5
PLANK #4
PLANK #3
PLANK #2
PLANK #1

6 7/8"
3 1/8"
15/16"
SCARF
6 3/8"
1/2"

STRING LINE

PLANK TOUCHES STRING

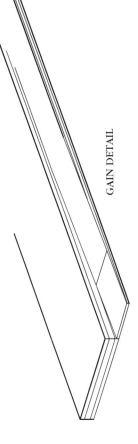

GAIN DETAIL

PLANK ALIGNMENT

1. EACH OF THE 10 HULL PLANKS ARE 2 SECTIONS.

2. STRETCH A STRING LINE ON THE FLOOR OR LONG WORK-
BENCH AND POSITION THE PLANKS ON THE STRING LINE AS
SHOWN.

3. AT EACH SCARF LOCATION CHECK THAT THE PLANK EDGE IS
THE INDICATED DISTANCE FROM THE STRING LINE.

4. ONCE THE PLANKS ARE ALIGNED PROPERLY, SECURE THEM
FROM MOVING. SPREAD GLUE ON THE SCARFS AND CLAMP THEM
AS SHOWN ON THE NEXT PAGE.

Sheet 2

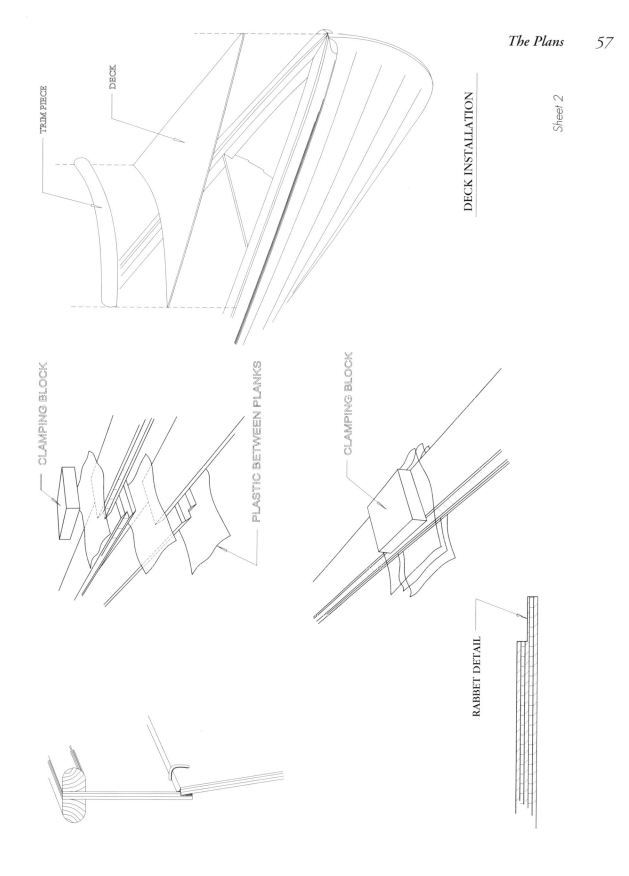

TRIM PIECE

DECK

DECK INSTALLATION

Sheet 2

CLAMPING BLOCK

PLASTIC BETWEEN PLANKS

CLAMPING BLOCK

RABBET DETAIL

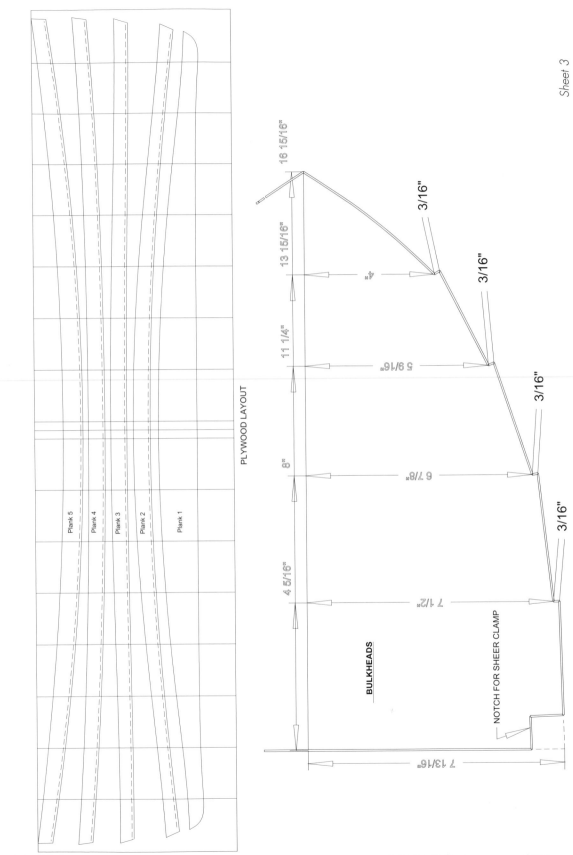

PLYWOOD LAYOUT

Plank 5
Plank 4
Plank 3
Plank 2
Plank 1

BULKHEADS

NOTCH FOR SHEER CLAMP

16 15/16"
13 15/16"
11 1/4"
8"
4 5/16"

4"
5 9/16"
6 7/8"
7 1/2"
7 13/16"

3/16"
3/16"
3/16"
3/16"

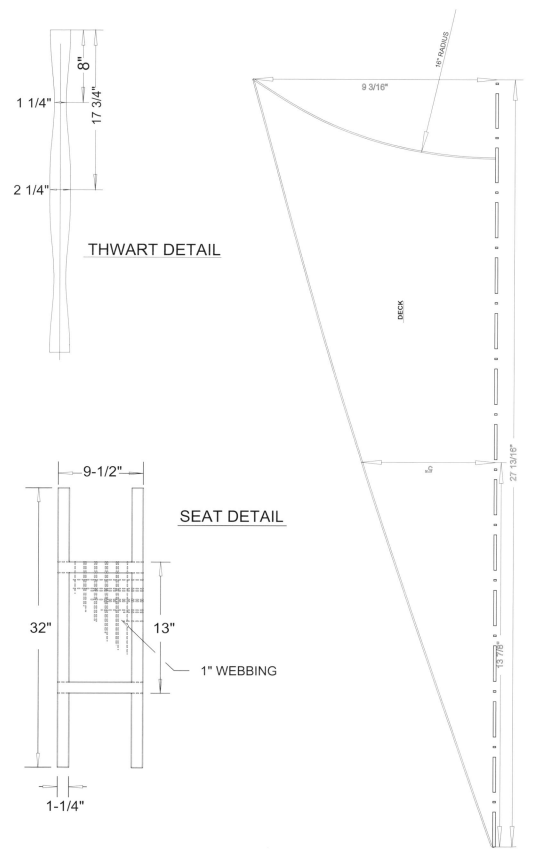

THWART DETAIL

8"

17 3/4"

1 1/4"

2 1/4"

SEAT DETAIL

9-1/2"

32"

13"

1" WEBBING

1-1/4"

9 3/16"

16" RADIUS

DECK

27 13/16"

5"

13 7/8"

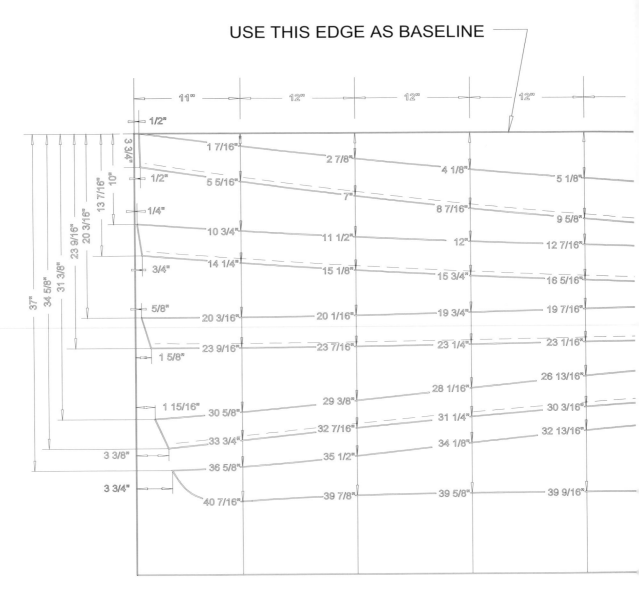

USE THIS EDGE AS BASELINE

STATION 1

1" SQUARES

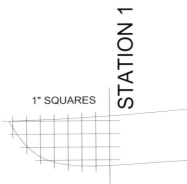

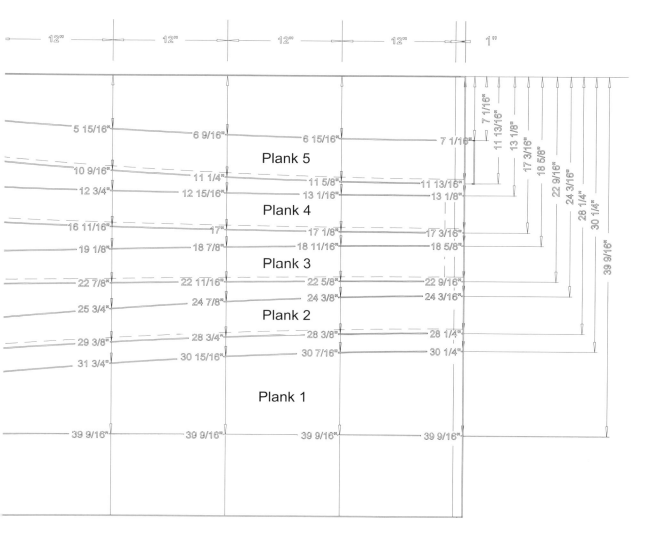

12"	12"	12"	12"	1"

5 15/16"   6 9/16"   6 15/16"   7 1/16"   7 1/16"

Plank 5

10 9/16"   11 1/4"   11 5/8"   11 13/16"   11 13/16"

12 3/4"   12 15/16"   13 1/16"   13 1/8"   13 1/8"

Plank 4

16 11/16"   17"   17 1/8"   17 3/16"   17 3/16"

19 1/8"   18 7/8"   18 11/16"   18 5/8"   18 5/8"

Plank 3

22 7/8"   22 11/16"   22 5/8"   22 9/16"   22 9/16"

25 3/4"   24 7/8"   24 3/8"   24 3/16"   24 3/16"

Plank 2

29 3/8"   28 3/4"   28 3/8"   28 1/4"   28 1/4"

31 3/4"   30 15/16"   30 7/16"   30 1/4"   30 1/4"

Plank 1

39 9/16"   39 9/16"   39 9/16"   39 9/16"   39 9/16"

SASSAFRAS 16 PANEL LAYOUT   *Sheet 4*

(continued from page 45)

Sassafras 16

This is the largest of the Sassafras canoes. At 15 feet, 8 inches long and with a 36-inch beam, it's large enough for all but serious trippers. With a weight of only 65 pounds, this is a comfortable boat to carry, and one person can easily lift it onto even a tall vehicle's roof rack. If using light backpacking-type gear, a trip of one or even two weeks is possible in the Sassafras 16. It tracks well and has enough height, or freeboard, to feel secure on fairly open water. The plans are on pages 54–61.

The Sassafras is stable enough for a person with good balance to stand and cast a fishing line—in calm water, that is. And, if the paddler is in the forward seat facing toward the stern, it handles well for a solo paddler. I think this is a particularly good-looking boat; the proportions came out just right.

The Sassafras 16 is built from 6 mm plywood and is a rugged craft. Although larger than the other boats, the 16-footer is just as simple to build.

Sassafras 16 Bill of Materials

- 5 sheets 6 mm BS1088 okoume marine plywood
- 1½ gallons marine-grade epoxy (total quantity of resin plus hardener)
- ½ gallon (by volume) wood-flour thickener for epoxy
- ½ gallon (by volume) silica thickener for epoxy
- 6 yards of 6-ounce, 50-inch-wide fiberglass cloth
- 250 feet of 18-gauge bare copper single-strand wire
- 4 pieces ¾-inch-square by 16-foot, 6-inch ash, mahogany, or other hardwood for inwales and outwales
- 36-inch canoe thwart or hardwood to make your own
- 4 #10 by 1¼-inch stainless steel wood screws or 2 stainless steel ¼- by 1¾-inch bolts, washers, and nuts for mounting thwart
- Hardwood to make deck trim pieces and doublers for hanging seats (see plan dimensions)
- 2 commercial canoe seats or materials to make one of the seat types shown in chapter 9
- 2 commercial seat-hanging kits or spacers and bolts as described in chapter 9

Even two large adults are comfortable in the Sassafras 16.

CHAPTER FIVE

▶ *Making the Panels*

Since there are no frames in our boats and they are not built on a mold, the shape of the planks that make up the hull defines the shape of the boat. The exact shape of each plank has been determined, as I explained in chapter 1, using a sophisticated computer program. As most of us lack computer-controlled cutters, we'll need to transfer, or lay out, the shape of each plank from the plan to a sheet of plywood. And we'll need to do this with great care and accuracy.

You've probably noticed that canoes are longer than a sheet of plywood. Two lengths of plywood will be joined to make a full-length plank. The joint we'll use is an overlapping bevel, or *scarf*. Traditionally the builder would stagger these scarfs along the boat's length. But, because the Sassafras canoes are symmetrical fore and aft, I've designed them with the joints exactly amidships. This allows the builder to lay out only one-quarter of the boat, rather than one-half of the boat as is usual in boatbuilding. In other words, the Sassafras canoe is composed of ten planks or five pairs of planks. One port and one

identical starboard plank make up each pair. And the planks are symmetrical around the boat's midpoint; the forward half of each plank is identical in shape to the aft half. So, we need to draw only half of one plank full size on an 8-foot piece of plywood. Then we can stack four layers of plywood and, using the first as a pattern, cut out four identical half-planks. Finally, we'll cut the scarf joints at the ends of each of the four half-planks, and glue them together to make a pair of full-length planks.

Laying Out the Hull Planks

Sheet 4 of the plans is a layout diagram showing the exact dimensions of each of the five planks. Actually, the dimensions given are for half of each plank, because that's all we'll need.

This diagram shows coordinates, as on a map, though we boatbuilders call them *offsets*. Offsets define points a given distance along a baseline, then a given distance at a right angle to the baseline. The

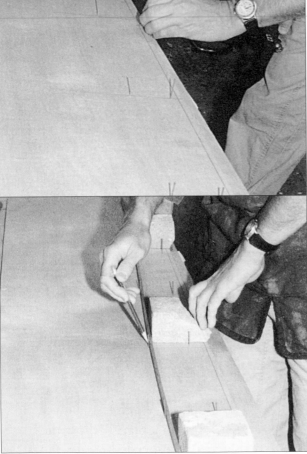

ABOVE: *Bill measures from the baseline to each off-set and makes a pencil mark. He uses a carpenter's square to ensure that the measurement is square to the baseline.* **LEFT:** *Bill drives a brad at each offset mark.* **BOTTOM:** *Then he uses a batten to draw a smooth curve between the brads. The batten is held against the brads with Bill's special boatbuilder's bricks.*

Sassafras plans use the top edge of the plywood sheet as the baselines.

The layout scheme in the plans does not make the most efficient use of the plywood—there is considerable waste—but it does make the task of laying out the panels very simple, which is more important for the novice builder. It's possible to redraw this diagram to make more efficient use of the plywood; experienced boatbuilders may want to do this. They might also cut templates for each plank from cardboard or inexpensive ⅛-inch plywood and then rearrange the templates on the okoume panels before tracing them and cutting the planks. But I'll assume you're using the layout diagram as shown in the plans.

To make the planks, you'll transfer the measurements to your plywood sheet; then you'll connect them with a curved line, thus drawing the planks. It's best to work on the floor or on a long bench; the panel should not droop off the end of your work surface. Measure down the edge of the plywood and mark off the 1-foot intervals, or *stations*, for each offset. Now measure offset distance below the baseline; that is, the distance from the baseline to the edge of the plank. Use your carpenter's square to draw a light line perpendicular to the baseline to ensure that you're measuring at a right angle. Mark the offset distances to both the bottom edge and the top edge of the panel with a small penciled cross. After you've laid out all the points, double-check them—this is important.

Now connect the offset points with a batten. The batten is used like a flexible straightedge to help you draw the edge of the panel. Drive a small brad at each measurement point. Hold the batten against the brads with clamps or weights such as bricks, rocks, or draftsman's lead ducks. Take your time adjusting the batten and weights to ensure a fair curve: a curve without any bumps, kinks, flat spots, or hollow areas. The only way I know to judge the fairness of a curve is just to stare down it for a while, as if sighting down a rifle barrel. When you're satisfied that your batten is lying in a truly fair line, pencil in the curve. If the batten seems unfair, or if it doesn't touch one of the brads, recheck the offsets.

You'll need to draw a tight curve at the end of the #1 plank. The full-size plans contain a full-size pattern for this.

But if you're working only from this book, you'll have to draw the curve by eye. The exact shape of this curve is not critical, but do try to get it close to what's shown on the plans.

Cutting Out the Planks

With the planks laid out and all the measurements double-checked, it's time to cut. You can use a handsaw, a saber saw, or a circular saw to cut the planks. If using a saber saw, fit it with a fresh 10-tooth-per-inch woodcutting blade. If using a circular saw, fit a fine-toothed crosscut blade and set the depth of cut to no more than the total thickness of the uncut plywood sheets, or *blanks*. Wear safety glasses while cutting so you won't be temporarily blinded by a puff of sawdust. Remember not to cut through the sections of plywood you'll need for the decks and bulkheads.

You'll cut the half-planks by stacking the four sheets of plywood, with the sheet showing the layout on top, and cutting through them all at once. This will ensure that the four half-planks that make up each pair of planks are identical.

Lay the plywood stack on your workbench with the layout line you'll cut first just over bench's edge. Clamp or nail the stack together so it won't shift as you cut. Don't try to cut the panels exactly to the layout line. If you have a steady hand, try to stay about $1/16$ inch outside it; if you've never used a saw, aim for $1/8$ inch or more outside it. Later you'll trim the panels exactly to the line with a plane. Allow the saw to find its best speed through the

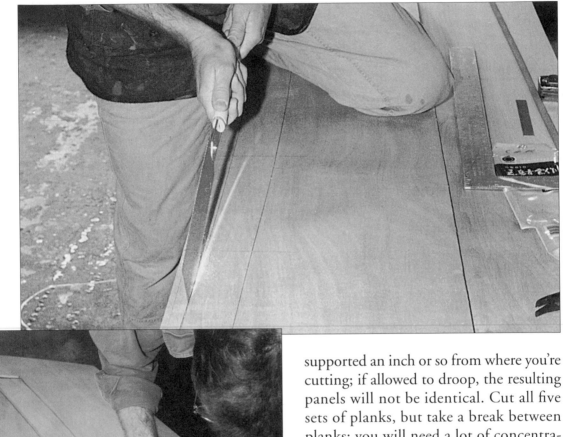

TOP: *You could cut out all the planks with a Japanese hand-saw; it's great exercise.* BOTTOM: *It's much faster to cut planks with a saber saw (or a circular saw).*

supported an inch or so from where you're cutting; if allowed to droop, the resulting panels will not be identical. Cut all five sets of planks, but take a break between planks; you will need a lot of concentration to follow a long curve with a saw.

You'll remove the last bit of wood with a block plane instead of a saw because you're less likely to cut beyond the line with the plane. Also, a plane leaves a fairer curve and a smoother edge. It's important to keep the plane sharp and not set too deep for this operation. This may seem to be a tedious step, but the plank edges can be planed within an hour or two.

When you plane your planks, remember that the two sides of the boat must absolutely, positively, and without doubt be identical. If they aren't, your canoe will pull to one side; at least you won't get lost in the fog. So support your panels to prevent them from drooping off the edge of your

wood; don't push it so fast that the motor slows. You might find it easier to use two hands to guide a saber saw. Keep moving the panel on the workbench so it's always

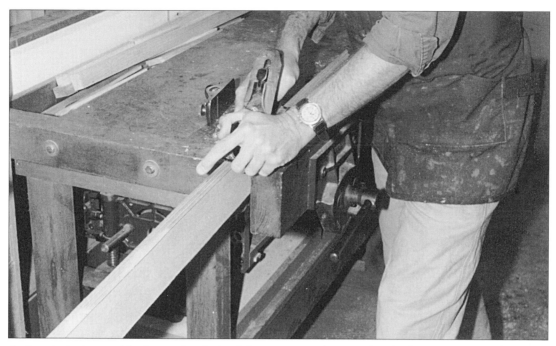

A plane is the best tool for fairing the planks. Bill is using a medium-size bench plane.

workbench; if they were to droop, the top panel would come out slightly larger than the bottom panel. Try to keep your plane perpendicular to the panels so as not to plane more from one edge than the other. Take long strokes, and, when you get close to the pencil line, stop often to sight down the plank, making sure the edge is fair. It's easy to get carried away and plane a flat spot. For this reason it's better to plane to the outside of the pencil line rather than to its inside. When you've finished planing the planks, lay the stacks on your shop floor and check them with a square, as shown in the photo on page 72, to be sure that they're identical.

Cutting the Scarfs

A scarf is simply a bevel or ramp cut into the end of the plank. With modern epoxy and plywood, the scarf should have an 8:1 ratio; that is, the length of the scarf should be eight times the thickness of the wood. The long length of the scarf provides sufficient gluing area to ensure that the joint is at least as strong as the surrounding wood.

An overlapping bevel, or scarf, is the best way to join thin plywood panels.

Start by marking a pencil line at the inside edge of the scarf to be cut. Because you'll be cutting an 8:1 scarf, this line will be 1¼ inches from the edge when joining 4 mm plywood (4 mm multiplied by 8 is 32 mm, or about 1¼ inches). In joining 6 mm plywood, the scarf line will be 2 inches from the edge. Make this line at the edge to be joined of each half-plank.

Cutting Scarfs with a Plane

The simplest way to cut a scarf is with a plane. Once again, check that your plane is sharp; try it out on a piece of scrap plywood. The glue in plywood quickly dulls plane irons, so you'll need to resharpen after you've cut a few scarfs. Set your blade for a shallow cut. You might think you'll save time by planing off great swaths of wood all at once, but sooner or later you'll

tear out a big chunk and perhaps ruin the panel.

Place one of the planks with its edge exactly on the edge of your workbench, scarf line up. If the edge of your workbench is worn and scarred, first tack down a good surface, such as a piece of scrap plywood. Hold the plank in place with a clamp. Now, plane away the wood between your pencil line and the bottom edge of the plank where it meets the edge of your workbench. Hold the plane at a slight angle and slowly cut along the edge of the plywood. As a "ramp" is formed, the layers in the plywood will appear as bands; try to keep these bands parallel as you plane. When you have a smooth, flat surface between your pencil line and a featherlike edge against the workbench, you're done.

Line up the planks like stair steps. This guides the plane at the correct angle, making cutting four scarfs at once easier than cutting them individually.

ABOVE: *Bill cuts scarfs for our Sassafras 16 with a block plane.* RIGHT: *The almost-finished scarfs show the layers of wood and glue in the plywood. Try to keep the bands parallel as you plane.*

It is both easier and faster to cut scarfs on all four identical half-planks at once. Position the planks flush with the edge of your workbench. Slide the top panel back so that its edge rests on the pencil line of the panel below it; stagger the remaining planks in this way and clamp them to your workbench. Now you can cut a ramp between the pencil line on the top sheet and the edge of the work-bench just as you would with a single sheet. Cutting scarfs with a block plane is probably easier to do than to explain. Practice on a piece of scrap, and you'll soon get the hang of it.

OTHER WAYS TO CUT SCARFS

Professional boatbuilders have devised several timesaving methods for cutting scarfs. Bill sometimes cuts scarfs with a

belt sander. The technique is similar to us-ing a block plane. He marks the edge of the scarf and staggers the panels at the edge of the bench. He sands away the wood to form a ramp. If you try this method, be sure to hold the sander so the belt runs "down" the ramp, not up it or sideways to it, to prevent tears. It's easy to sand off too much wood, so work slowly. An 80-grit sanding belt seems best for cut-ting scarfs.

A method I've used to cut scarfs is with a router and jig. The router is fitted with a wide mortising bit and mounted on a short board. The board, with the attached router, slides up and down a frame set at the proper angle to cut an 8:1 scarf. The frame or jig fits over the plywood panel to be scarfed, and you need only push the router along to cut a perfect scarf. The only drawback of this method is that you must set everything up, and setup can take as long as cutting the scarf with a plane or belt sander. Of course, a production shop could dedicate a router and table exclusively to scarfing and have a very efficient system.

Gluing the Planks

Before the planks are glued, they must be aligned; sheet 2 of the plans contains a diagram to help you align them. The planks should be glued on a long, flat surface. Because most of us don't have workbenches that are long enough, we'll probably glue them on the floor. It's convenient to drive some brads or staples into the work surface to hold the planks in alignment, so you might lay a couple of sheets of scrap plywood over a concrete or polished hardwood floor. Start by snapping a baseline with your chalkline, or stretching a string, on the surface where you'll glue the planks. Lay the first set of planks above the baseline or string as shown in the plans; check the offset shown at the center of the scarf. Also check that the scarfs are properly overlapped. Take your time here; the alignment of the planks is critical. Bill sometimes traces the properly aligned planks on the work surface to make them easy to check, should they slip while the scarfs are being glued. Lay the second identical pair of half-planks on top of the first and secure the stack to the work surface with a couple of small nails or heavy weights at the ends.

Gently lift the stack of planks at the middle and slide a piece of wax paper or plastic film under the bottom scarf. Mix an ounce or two of epoxy and thicken it with silica powder to the consistency of jam. You should always be extra careful when gluing scarf joints. Check that the

Measure the distance from the baseline to the scarf when aligning the planks for gluing as shown in the alignment drawing in the plans.

temperature is within the epoxy manufacturer's specifications and that the resin and hardener are mixed to exactly the right ratio. Then double-check that the panels are perfectly aligned. Ask an assistant to lift the planks to expose the bottom scarf joint and spread epoxy on both surfaces of the joint. Place a piece of plastic or wax paper on the top plank, and spread epoxy on the second scarf joint. Cover this joint with a sheet of wax paper or plastic.

Clamping a scarf joint can be tricky. With these narrow planks, C-clamps will do the job if you're fortunate enough to be working on the edge of a long workbench. Be sure to place a wooden pad over the joint to spread the load of the clamp evenly. Don't overtighten the clamps; some epoxy should squeeze out of the joint and the surfaces should touch, but too much pressure will squeeze all the epoxy from the scarf, making a weak joint.

Triple-check the alignment and the overlap of the scarfs because the pressure of clamping a scarf joint often causes the plywood to slide apart.

For most of us, working on a floor, there are other methods of clamping. One way is by placing a scrap of wood, at least ½ inch thick, over the joint and driving a screw just beyond the edge of the planks as shown in the photo. You can also clamp scarfs with heavy weights, such as 5-gallon buckets of water. Be sure to secure the ends so the panels don't slide apart when the weight is placed on the joint. Place a piece of wax paper, then a block of wood, over the scarf. The block of wood should be slightly longer and wider than the scarf joint; this ensures that all the weight will be concentrated on the joint. Balance the weight on the block and check that the panels have not slipped out of alignment.

Bill uses a block of scrap wood and two drywall screws to clamp each scarf joint. Notice the plastic sheet that prevents the block from adhering to the plank.

Join all five pairs of panels this way and allow the epoxy to cure overnight or longer. When you can no longer press a fingernail into the epoxy, remove the clamps, weights, nails, or screws. Most scarf joints will require a little sanding to remove the glue that has squeezed out of the joint. Sand them carefully so you don't remove any wood. I prefer to leave a little epoxy on the surface, rather than risk sanding into the plank. Handle the planks with care; the epoxy has not reached full strength yet.

TOP: *All the planks for the Sassafras 16 (stacked in pairs). To the right are the inwales and outwales, which have also been scarfed. Bill has cut the rabbets before gluing the planks; most builders glue the planks first.* **BOTTOM:** *Sand off the epoxy that has squeezed out of the scarf joint, but try not to remove any wood.*

Cutting the Rabbets

We can cut rabbets with a rabbet plane or with a router. Remember that the rabbets are on the inside bottom edge of each plank except the bottom, or #1, plank. They are ⅜ inch wide and about ¹⁄₁₆ inch deep. Actually the exact depth is not terribly important. The rabbet should be deep enough so the planks lock together when they are wired, but too deep a rabbet reduces strength. I like to make the depth

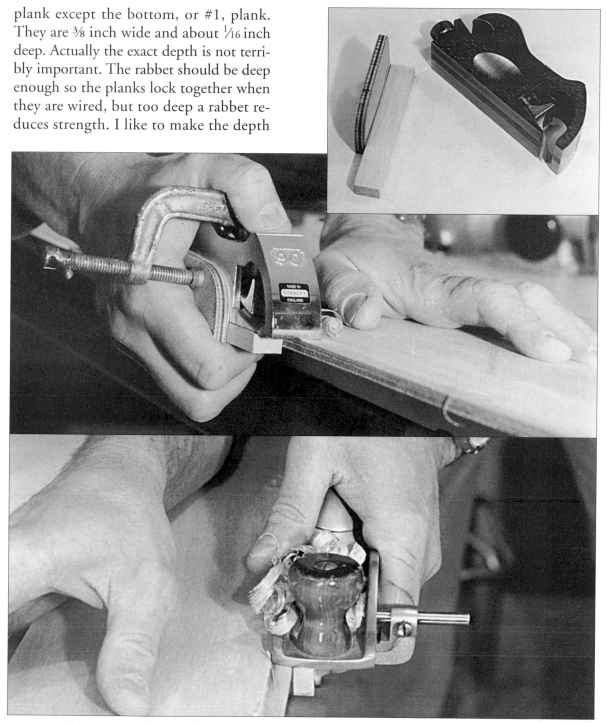

TOP RIGHT: *The Stanley model 90 bullnose plane and a homemade rabbeting fence.*
MIDDLE: *Cutting a rabbet with the model 90 and homemade fence.* BOTTOM: *This Lie-Nielsen plane has a removable fence.*

The router makes short work of cutting the rabbets.

The cutter on the ⅜-inch rabbeting bit should extend about ¹⁄₁₆ inch beyond the router's base.

about the same as the thickness of one layer of the plywood. This makes it easy to cut a consistently deep rabbet; just stop planing when the first glue line is exposed.

Cutting rabbets with a plane requires a fence. A fence is simply a block that limits the width of the rabbet and guides the plane along the edge of the plank. Some planes, such as the Lie-Nielsen and Record 778, come with fences, and you need only adjust them to leave ⅜ inch of the plane's sole exposed. If you're using a bullnose plane, make an L-shaped rabbeting fence by gluing a block of the proper width (one that leaves ⅜ inch of plane iron exposed) to

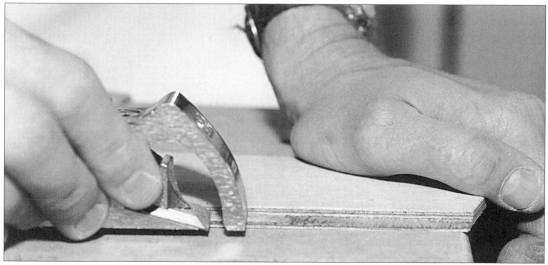

Cutting gains is simply a matter of making a scarflike taper in the last 4 inches of the rabbet.

a scrap of plywood, as shown in the bottom photo on page 73. Clamp the fence to the body of the plane.

Lay the plank on the edge of your workbench, and, using the fence as a guide, cut a rabbet along the entire bottom inside edge. By the way, the inside face of the plank can be either side; I choose the side with prettier grain because I like to varnish the inside of a boat and paint the outside.

If you have a router, fit the ⅜-inch rabbeting bit and adjust the depth of cut to about ¹⁄₁₆ inch. These bits have a bearing that rides on the outside edge of the plank; the cutter overhangs the bearing by ⅜ inch. Try the router on a scrap of plywood first; it may take a few tries to get the depth just right. If the rabbet looks good, clamp each plank to the edge of the workbench and cut the rabbets. Remember, the bottom, or #1, plank doesn't have a rabbet.

Cutting the Gains

Gains are tapers in the planks at the ends of the rabbets. They allow the overlapping strakes to blend together at the bow and stern. This looks nice and is traditional on lapstrake craft. The gains on the Sassafras canoe's planks should be about 4 inches long.

If using a rabbet or bullnose plane, simply taper the last 4 inches of the rabbets into a scarflike ramp. If you cut the rabbet with a router and don't have a rabbet plane, use a sanding block to make the gains. The inside corner of the gains should be square, but if cut with a sanding block, it will be somewhat rounded. In this case, square up the corner with a sharp chisel or razor knife.

CHAPTER SIX

▶*Assembling the Hull*

This is the fun part. In just a few hours, your carefully shaped planks will become a canoe. Before you start assembling them, examine each plank carefully. Clean up any epoxy drips with your plane or coarse sandpaper, and be certain that the rabbets and curves are smooth and fair.

Experienced boatbuilders have probably noticed that I refer to "planks" rather than "strakes," which is the correct term when describing a lapstrake boat. I also refer to the planks by number, #1 being the bottommost plank and #5 being the topmost plank. Technically, the #1 plank is called the *garboard plank*; the next plank is the *first broad plank*. The *second broad plank* follows it, and then we have the *third broad plank*. The topmost plank is not called the fourth broad plank, as you might expect; it is the *sheer plank*. So you see why I've simplified things.

Joining the Planks

We'll start by joining all the planks with copper wire twisted through holes in the planks' edges. Drill ⅟₁₆-inch holes, ½ inch in from the edge, every 6 inches along the perimeter of the two #1 planks. Stack the two planks when drilling so the holes will be in the same position on both planks and drill the holes along both edges. It's best to drill the holes with the planks resting on the workbench or on a piece of scrap wood to prevent the wood from splintering where the drill bit exits.

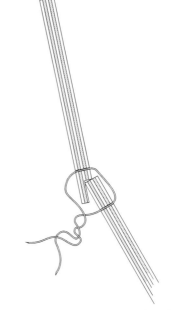

The wire holes should be positioned so the wire pulls the lower plank firmly into the rabbet.

Also drill holes, at the same spacing, along only the top edges of the #2, #3, and #4 planks, but not in the #5 planks. We'll drill the holes on the adjacent edges, the bottom edges, as we join the planks, because the holes' positions will shift slightly as each plank is bent to shape.

Bill's drilling guide, shown in the photo, is handy for this step. It's nothing more than a piece of wood 1 inch wide and about 7 inches long, with two holes drilled 6 inches apart and ½ inch from the ends. Place the drill bit in one of the holes in the guide and drill the first hole. Before pulling out the bit, swivel the guide about the bit to locate the next hole. Hold the guide in its new position while you move the drill bit to the second hole in the guide. Drill the new hole, swivel the guide, and so on.

When all holes are drilled, place the two #1 planks on your sawhorses. Connect them along the keel line using pieces of copper wire about 4 inches long. With your pliers, twist the wires loosely on the outside of the hull. Try to twist all the wires in the same direction, clockwise or counterclockwise, to save time when tightening or loosening them later.

Bill's drilling guide locates the wire holes at the edges of the planks.

LEFT: *Join the #1 planks along the keel line, then open them like a book.* **RIGHT:** *Stitching the #2 planks to the #1 planks.*

Next, wire the #2 planks to the #1 planks. Line up the ends of the planks and, starting at one end, drill a hole in the bottom edge of the #2 plank that corresponds to the hole in the #1 plank. The new hole should be just above the rabbet; if the hole is correctly placed, the wire will pull the #1 plank firmly into the rabbet. Join the panels with a piece of wire and drill the next hole. Continue joining the #2 planks to the #1 planks, drilling holes as you go and leaving the twists on the outside. But don't overtighten the wires;

the planks must continue to bend and shift as the rest of the parts are added. You'll notice that the planks don't seem to meet properly near their ends. The hull will be joined at the stems, or ends of the boat, causing the planks to twist as the ends of the planks are brought into alignment; for now leave the wires loose.

Attach the #3, the #4, and finally the #5 planks in the same manner, starting at one end and drilling as you go. The hull will start to take shape and no longer lie flat on the sawhorses. The shape of the

ABOVE: *Don't overtighten the wires, or you'll distort the planks.* **RIGHT:** *The #5 planks go on last* **BOTTOM:** *Notice that the ends of the planks don't fit until the hull is brought together at the stems.*

canoe won't appear until all the wires are in and tight; for now, just try to get all the planks into place and don't worry about the shape.

When all the planks are joined along their lengths, drill two holes in the end of each plank, one above the other, and pull the planks together at the bow and stern. This can be a fight, particularly on a 6 mm hull; you're twisting the bottom planks almost 90 degrees, and it's hard to hold them in position with one hand while threading the wires with the other. It will probably require an assistant to hold the planks while you wire them together. In fact, I had to put down my camera and hold the planks for Bill while building the boat in this book. If you don't have a helper, use spring clamps to position the plank ends.

ABOVE: *Bringing the planks into a line and stitching them at the stems can be a struggle.* **LEFT:** *A spreader stick brings the hull to its proper beam. Make the spreader stick ½ inch shorter than the beam given on the plans.*

When the ends of all the planks are joined, cut a spreader stick from scrap wood to spread the hull to its eventual beam; the stick's length should equal the boat's beam less ½ inch. Insert the spreader stick amidships to bring the hull to its proper width. Secure the spreader stick with a brad or small nail passing through the plank into the end of the stick; the gunwale will cover the nail hole.

Now check that the hull is symmetrical. If the planks are misaligned by even a quarter of an inch, the boat could pull to one side. Check that the pairs of hull panels, which you previously ascertained were identical in length and alignment,

ABOVE: *Bill taps the planks to bring them into alignment.* RIGHT: *Two scrap wood cleats keep the planks straight at the bow and stern.*

meet evenly at the bow and stern—that is, one panel doesn't extend past its mate. If a plank does stick out, tap it with a mallet. If this doesn't bring it into position, loosen the wires and slide the plank back. After considerable tapping and sliding, the planks will be perfectly aligned at the bow and stern.

Also check that the stems are straight. Sight down the stems from above; do the ends of the planks zigzag a little? If they do, clamp or screw two pieces of scrap wood on the bow to keep the planks aligned, as shown in the photo at right. Take care that you don't overtighten the clamps and pinch or distort the stems.

When the planks are aligned, tighten the wires, but be careful not to distort the planks.

With the planks assembled and checked, gently turn the hull upside down and tighten all the wires. It may take some pressure to draw the planks together near the ends of the hull, but generally it's necessary only to snug the wires. Overtightening them will make dents in the planks that require lots of sanding later on. If the planks touch and are pulled into the bottom of the rabbets, the wires are tight enough.

Making and Installing the Bulkheads

The bulkheads are the "walls" that form the canoe's flotation compartments. They also serve to shape the boat's ends. Cut the bulkheads from the leftover plywood from the planks. Refer to the bulkhead draw-ing in the plans and draw a centerline and a baseline on the plywood. Measure up from the baseline, then over at right angles to the centerline to establish the shape of the bulkheads. The pattern and dimensions in the plans show only half the bulkhead, but you'll make measurements to both sides of the centerline when laying them out. Don't forget to cut the notches for the inwales.

The positions of the bulkheads are shown on the plans, though you can move them an inch or so to get a better fit. You'll need to pull in, or pinch, the hull slightly to make a tight fit to the bulkheads. Fitting bulkheads is one of the harder chores in boatbuilding; even with computer design they rarely seem to fit exactly right.

If the bulkheads simply won't fit well, scribe and trim them. Hold a pencil flat

ABOVE: *Scribe the bulkheads by holding a pencil flat against the hull. This will ensure a perfect fit.*
RIGHT: *Wire the bulkheads into place.*

against the hull and make a line on the bulkhead that traces the hull's shape. Cut the bulkhead to the line and recheck the fit. You might need to scribe the bulkheads two or three times to get a perfect fit. Of course, this process makes the bulkhead smaller and moves it toward the end of the hull. But the exact position of the bulkheads is not important, nor is the exact angle of the bulkhead. So feel free to adjust it for best fit.

When you're satisfied with their fit, wire the bulkheads into position. Drill holes and pass a wire through the plank, through the bulkhead, and out through the plank again. Try to keep the plank holes and wires close to the bulkhead. Push the wires down inside the hull with a screwdriver so they lie flat against the wood. Check that the bulkheads don't push out on the hull, causing a bulge or lump in the planking. It's preferable that the bulkheads are slightly loose, rather than too tight. An epoxy fillet will later cover any gap between the bulkheads and the planks.

You may notice in the photographs that Bill and I installed the bulkheads after gluing the hull. You'd think that a professional boatbuilder and a professional boat designer would have the sense to follow their own directions. Well, we thought our new method might be easier; it turned out to be more trouble and a lot more time-consuming. In the future, we'll go back to placing bulkheads only after wiring the planks, as you should.

CHAPTER SEVEN

▶*Gluing the Hull*

Now that your creation looks like a canoe, we'll join the parts permanently with epoxy. Then we'll install the inwales and outwales, which make up the gunwales. And then your hull will be completed. Before gluing, check one last time that the planks fit as perfectly as possible, that they meet evenly along the keel line, and that the stems are straight.

This is the first step in which we'll use large quantities of epoxy, so remember that epoxy drips and runs are much easier to wipe off when wet than to sand off when rock hard. And pay careful attention to the resin-to-hardener ratio.

Making Fillets

A fillet is a bead of thickened epoxy at the inside juncture of two parts. The fillets form structural members that replace wooden parts in traditional wooden boats. On our canoes, they'll join the planks at the ends of the boat, replacing wooden stems, and secure the bulkheads to the hull, replacing screws and frames.

By the way, it's pronounced "fill-it," not "fill-lay."

To make the fillet mixture, thicken about 8 ounces of epoxy with wood flour. Remember to mix the epoxy resin and hardener thoroughly before adding the thickening powder. Mix in enough wood flour to make a paste of about the consistency of peanut butter—smooth supermarket peanut butter, not chunky style. If the mix is too thin, it'll run and pool at the bottom of the boat. If it's too thick, it'll pull, leave gaps, and not adhere to the plywood. So how do you know if you have the right consistency? Mix a few ounces and try it; if it's too thick or thin, scrape it off and try again. We use wood flour because it makes a stiff, strong mix that's easy to shape and is thick and sticky enough to adhere to the wood, staying in place until it cures. Its dark brown color looks nice in a wooden boat. By adding a little white filler, such as silica, to the mix, you might even match the plywood color.

You'll need a few specialized tools for making fillets. Make two or three spread-

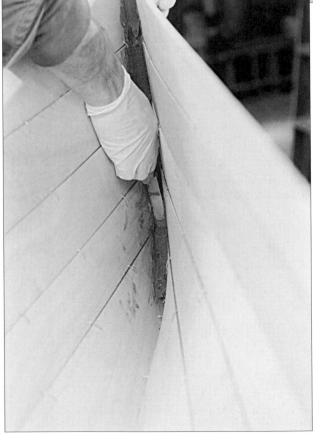

ABOVE: *A selection of specialized tools for making fillets.* **LEFT:** *Making a fillet in the stem.*

ers that look like Popsicle sticks, rounded at the ends and flat. Make them of different sizes and lengths from scrap plywood. You'll also need a plastic spreader or a putty knife. Some boatbuilders use an old soupspoon to shape fillets.

First we'll glue the planks along the stems with fillets at the bow and stern that stop at the bulkheads. Using a long Popsicle stick–shaped spreader, push the epoxy mix into both ends of the canoe, making a fillet about 1 inch wide. Extend the fillets along the keel line back to the bulkhead. Carefully scoop up any epoxy paste that squeezes past the sides of the spreader. It's nearly impossible to make neat fillets in the tight confines of a canoe's stems; fortunately, no one will see them once the deck is in place.

Cut two strips of fiberglass cloth 3

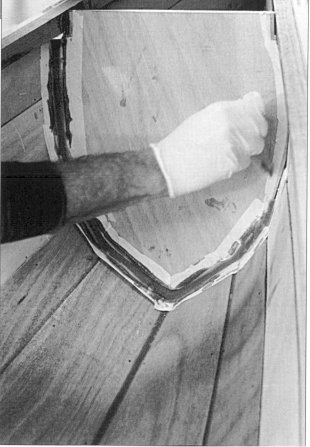

ABOVE: *The stem fillet extends back along the keel to the bulkhead. The bulkhead is joined to the hull with another fillet.* **RIGHT:** *Bill masks the fillet around the bulkhead with tape to keep excess epoxy off the surrounding wood.*

inches wide and long enough to cover the fillets you just made. Mix a few ounces of epoxy, but don't add any thickening powder. Lay the fiberglass strip on the fillets while they are still wet. Brush the epoxy onto the fiberglass, pushing out air bubbles and wrinkles. The fiberglass will become transparent and adhere to the fillet and surrounding wood.

With a smaller spreader stick, make a fillet along the perimeter of the bulkheads to join them to the hull. These fillets should be smaller, about ¾ inch wide. Make fillets on both sides of both bulkheads. The fillets on the outside faces of the bulkheads will be visible, so try to make them as neat as possible. Scrape off every bit of excess epoxy with a plastic spreader or putty knife. Some boatbuilders use masking tape to define the fillet and keep epoxy off the surrounding wood; of course, you must remove the tape, and excess epoxy, before the fillet hardens.

Gluing the Hull Seams

Once the stem fillets have cured, place the hull upside down on two level and parallel sawhorses. The sawhorses should be exactly perpendicular to the canoe; check this by measuring from the sawhorses to the spreader stick or bulkheads on both sides. This will ensure that there's no twist in the hull.

It should now be evident that you must fill all those narrow seams between the planks with epoxy. When developing this building method, I tried several techniques for getting the epoxy into the cracks. I knew that the strength of the hull depends on the epoxy penetrating to the very bottom of the joint, so I wanted to be

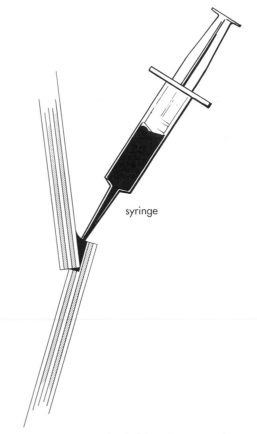

syringe

It's important to completely fill each seam with epoxy.

Use a small epoxy syringe to inject epoxy into the seams.

sure I could completely fill the seam without smearing thickened epoxy all over the hull. Brushing the stuff onto the hull and hoping it would flow into the seams was painfully slow and ineffective. I tried pouring it in from a paper cup, which resulted in a mess of drips and runs on the hull and rather crusty shoes. A sort of chef's pastry bag made from a clear plastic bag was far too much trouble. The solution is the inexpensive plastic syringe sold by many epoxy manufacturers. It is fast and simple to squirt the epoxy right into the seam and avoid dripping it on the hull. These syringes come in several sizes; I find the small size sold by West System best. By the way, many medical and veterinary supply houses carry plastic syringes, in case you don't have a local boatbuilding shop.

Mix about 8 ounces of epoxy and thicken it with silica to the consistency of thin gravy or salad dressing. The epoxy must be thin enough to flow into the confines of the joint. Cut about ¼ inch off the tip of a small epoxy syringe, making the opening larger. Suck some epoxy into the syringe—don't try to pour it in from the top—and inject it into each of the seams between the planks, filling them to almost overflowing. Move the syringe steadily along the seam as it fills, refilling the syringe as needed. Work quickly so the epoxy in the mixing cup doesn't harden.

Because it's crucial that the epoxy reach and fill the entire seam, you should spread or flex the seams near the ends of the hull where the seam becomes smaller. Use a knife blade or the tip of the syringe to flex the joint and ensure that the epoxy flows to the bottom of the seam. Capillary action will help draw the epoxy into the

joint. When I purposely broke test sections of LapStitch hulls, I found that they would snap at a seam only if the seam was not completely filled with epoxy. I also found, by cutting through test sections, that if a thin epoxy mixture was used and I was careful when injecting the epoxy, then almost all the seams would be full.

Mix more epoxy as needed and inject all the seams. Also fill the gap between the #1 panels along the keel. As the epoxy flows into the bottoms of the seams, add more as needed. This process is surprisingly fast; you can easily glue a 16-foot canoe in less than two hours.

Don't forget to fill the seam along the keel line.

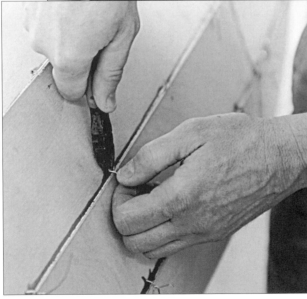

TOP: *Check under the boat for glue that may have leaked through; wipe up any that has.* BOTTOM: *After the epoxy in the hull seams has hardened, cut the tie wires and pull them out. Notice that the seams are completely filled with epoxy.*

Check under the boat to be sure that no epoxy has leaked through. If you find a leak, wipe up the epoxy immediately, rather than sand it off after it hardens. If it continues to leak, use masking tape to seal the seam. If the planks were accurately cut, though, there will be no leaks. When finished, don't forget to disassemble the syringe and wash it with solvent.

When the epoxy in the seams has hardened, cut and pull out all those wires you spent hours inserting. It will be difficult to pull out the wires along the stems and bulkheads, so cut these off with your diagonal wire cutters as close to the wood as possible, then sand or file the remaining nub flush.

The wood may have absorbed some of the epoxy you injected, so the seams still may not be full. Mix more epoxy, but add a little more thickener this time, and inject it into the seams where needed. When the seams are full, surface tension will cause the epoxy to "climb" the plank above, forming a small fillet above each seam. You may want to tool each seam with a small spreader to neaten the epoxy. Wipe up any overflow and allow the epoxy to harden; again, check that you can't dent the epoxy with a fingernail before proceeding.

The Inwales and Outwales

The inwales and outwales form the canoe's gunwales. The inwales go inside the hull, while the outwales, you guessed it, are glued to the outside. The Sassafras 12 and 14 canoes have ¾-inch-square inwales and outwales, while those on the Sassafras 16 are ¾ by 1 inch, with the 1-inch side glued to the hull. You can rip either size from a nominal 1-inch ash, mahogany, fir, or other strong flexible wood.

The inwales and outwales will be as long as the canoe, but you should start with pieces a few inches too long. You might need to join two pieces of wood to obtain the needed length; of course, you'll use a scarf joint. Because these solid parts are much thicker than plywood panels, the scarf joint will be longer. The scarf joint in our ¾-inch-thick wales will be 6 inches long. You could cut scarfs in solid wood with a plane as you did in the plywood panels. But to save time, cut away

If you can't find sufficiently long stock for the inwales and outwales, use scarf joints to join shorter pieces. These scarfs are 6 inches long.

A sliding jig for cutting scarfs in inwales and outwales.

the blade; that angle is 1 inch in 8 inches (or ¾ inch in 6 inches). The jig must slide with the wood, so it should ride in the miter gauge groove on the table. With a jig like the one in the photo, you'll be able to cut the scarfs in a set of inwales in a minute or two. After gluing the scarfs, allow the epoxy to cure for at least 12 hours, then sand off any epoxy that's squeezed out of the joint.

This is a good time to round over the corners of the outwales. If you have a router, fit it with a ¼-inch round-over bit and run down both outside corners of each outwale. Again, remember that the 1-inch-wide side will be glued to the hull on the 16-footer. Don't round the inwales yet. If you plan to round over the outwales with a plane or by sanding, it's just as easy to do it after they are attached to the hull.

Cut the outwales to precisely the right length by clamping them to the hull

most of the wood with a handsaw and finish up the ramp with your plane.

For those of you with table saws, there's an even easier way to cut scarfs in inwales and outwales. Make a wooden jig that holds the wood at the proper angle to

The inwales may be cut short, as on this canoe, thus eliminating the tricky bevel.

and cutting them off even with the stems. Because the inwales fit inside the hull, they are more difficult to trim to length. There are two ways to cut the inwales. My preferred method is to bevel them, as this makes for a slightly stronger boat. The other way is to cut the inwales 3 to 4 inches shorter than the boat so they don't quite reach the stems. With this second method, there is no need for a bevel; since the decks hide the ends of the inwales, no one can tell that you didn't make that tricky cut, unless they notice the very slight bump on the outside of the hull where the inwales end. If you choose to cut them off square, it's simple enough to ascertain their length by holding them against the top of the #5 plank and marking the required length.

If you decide to bevel the ends of the inwales, you'll need to determine the correct angle for the bevel. Do this by stretching a string or chalkline from stem to

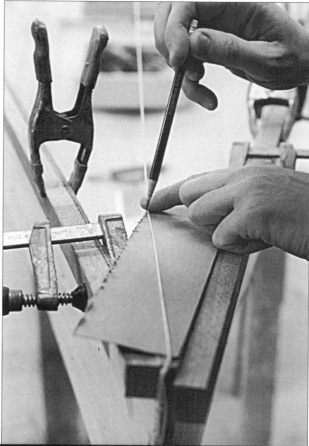

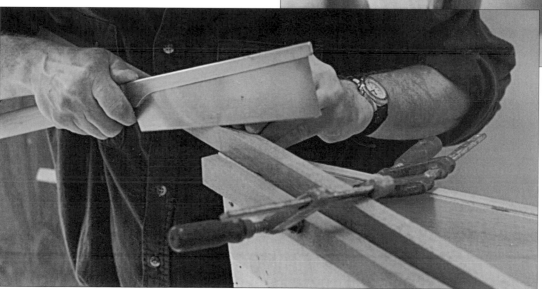

TOP: *Use a string line and a piece of cardboard to determine the bevel angle for the inwale.*
BOTTOM: *Bill cuts an inwale bevel.*

With a few spring clamps holding the wales in position, Bill taps one of the outwales to bring it level with the top of the #5 plank.

stem. Measure the angle between the string and the top of the #5 plank with a protractor or bevel gauge, or mark it on a piece of cardboard; leave the outwales clamped in place as you do this because they affect the bend of the top plank. Mark this angle on one end of the inwales and make the cut with your Japanese saw. Don't be concerned if you find that the angle is a little different at the bow and stern. It's best to cut the bevel a little proud and then plane it until the inwales fit together perfectly; try fitting them in

the boat. You'll need to trim a little off the pointy end to clear the fillet in the stem. Clamp the end of inwale into the hull; push the beveled end into position. Clamp the inwale into place as best you can; of course, the uncut end won't fit into the boat, but you can clamp and hold it just above the stem well enough to mark its length. With the length determined, cut the second bevel. Don't worry if a bevel doesn't fit perfectly; epoxy will fill any gap and the deck will hide it.

When you're satisfied with the fit of

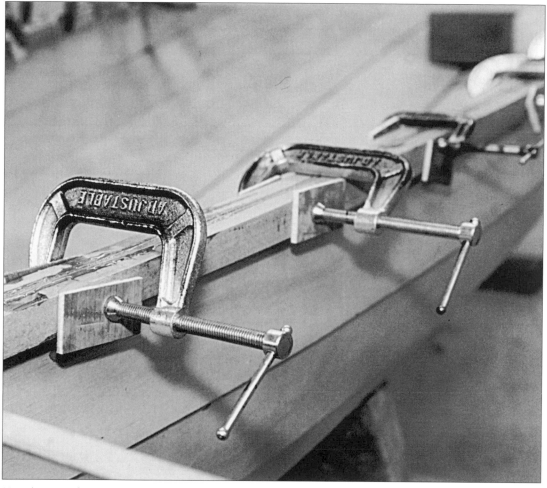

Use clamp pads to protect the wales from clamp dents.

the inwales, spread thickened epoxy along both the inwales and the outwales. Position them along the top edge of the planks and clamp them every 6 to 8 inches. This will be awkward if you're working alone, so ask your trusty assistant to hold the wales in place while you position the first few clamps. Be sure to use clamp pads— little squares of scrap plywood that prevent the clamps from denting the wales.

If you don't have enough clamps to glue in the inwales and outwales, you could secure them with 1½-inch bronze or stainless steel screws. These should be driven from the outside every 6 inches. To look right, the screws should be countersunk and the holes plugged with *bungs*, or wooden plugs. I know that many commercially made canoes have exposed screws along the gunwale, but that's one reason we're building our own canoe. If you decide to bung the screws, I recommend buying a matched bung cutter and drill bit to be sure the plugs fit tightly. Bung cutters are meant to fit in a drill press, but if you have a strong grip and pure thoughts, it's

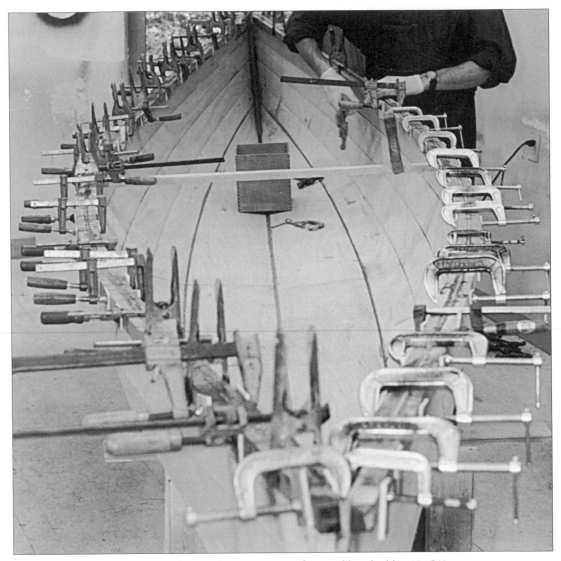

You, too, could have this many clamps, if you were a professional boatbuilder. It's OK to glue on one gunwale at a time.

possible to use them with a handheld drill. Woodworking catalogs sometimes sell pre-cut bungs, but the selection of woods is limited. Tradition dictates that the grain in the bungs run the same way as the grain in the outwales.

CHAPTER EIGHT

▶*Glassing the Bottom*

For hundreds of years, wooden canoes have been built with only paint, varnish, or canvas covering their bottoms. Today we can use fiberglass cloth set in epoxy to strengthen and stiffen the bottom of the hull and increase abrasion resistance. This type of covering will not make our craft as rugged as a plastic or Kevlar canoe, but it will better resist the unavoidable scratches and dings than wood alone. The fiberglass also connects and strengthens the seam along the keel line, which does not overlap like the other hull seams but is only a weak butt joint before it's glassed. We'll glass the bottom of the #1 planks and both the #1 and #2 planks on the inside of the hull. If your boat will see rough use, you can add additional fiberglass strips to the keel line.

Fiberglass cloth is nothing more than woven strands of the same material used in making windowpanes. At first thought, you might not believe this is strong enough; after all, a small rock can destroy a big window. But try to tear a piece of glass cloth—it's almost impossible. None-

theless, I am often asked about using even stronger cloths made of Kevlar, graphite, or other exotic fabrics instead of regular fiberglass, or E-glass as it's listed in catalogs. Not only is Kevlar expensive, but also it is difficult to work with and almost impossible to sand smooth. Graphite cloth is even more expensive and quite brittle; other fabrics present problems such as too much stretch or less weight than is suitable for these designs. Stick to regular fiberglass cloth.

Glassing the Exterior

Before glassing, lightly sand the outside of the hull with 80-grit paper if using an electric sander or with 120-grit paper if sanding by hand. This is not the final sanding, so don't overdo it. Your purpose is to remove any excess epoxy and splintering around the wire holes. Also, round over the keel area and the stems. The stems must be very smooth with no sharp corners; fiberglass won't lie on sharp edges.

The radius of each stem should be about as round as a fat fountain pen or a thin cigar. Take your time sanding the stems; they'll certainly stand out if they are not smooth and even. Also examine the stems from the side; they should describe a fair and pleasing curve as shown in the plans. Shape them with your plane if they don't look right. The curve of the stems is very important to the appearance of any boat. Designers spend hours getting those curves just so. It's worth spending a few extra minutes touching them up. Before going on, wipe or vacuum all the sanding dust off the hull, so as not to trap it under the fiberglass.

TOP: *Before fiberglassing, lightly sand the hull, inside and out.* BOTTOM: *Bill uses a file to clean up epoxy drips along the plank overlaps.*

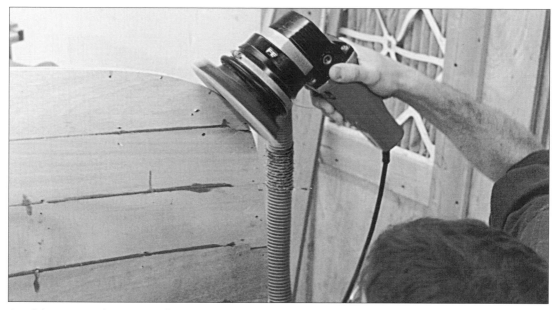

Sand the stems and pay special attention to their shape.

With the hull upside down on level sawhorses, mask off the #1 planks by applying masking tape along the bottom edge of the #2 planks. Mix a little epoxy and wood flour and fill the wire holes in the area to be glassed; actually, you might as well fill all the wire holes now. Use a plastic squeegee or putty knife to push the epoxy into each hole and wipe off all the excess, just like spackling a nail hole in drywall.

Spread your fiberglass cloth on a

With the wire holes filled and the #2 planks taped, the bottom is ready for fiberglass.

clean table or floor, and use sharp scissors to cut it into two strips. One strip should be a few inches wider than your canoe's #1 panels, the other strip should cover both the #1 and #2 panels. The small pieces of fiberglass needed for the stems will be cut from the ends and corners after we trim the strips to the shape of the panels.

Lay the narrower piece of fiberglass cloth on the overturned hull and trim it an inch or two wider than the #1 planks; it should reach just past the masking tape. Smooth the cloth by pulling it gently so it stretches to conform to the shape of the #1 planks. Check that there

are no loose threads, bits of balled-up epoxy, or pieces of sawdust under the cloth.

Mix about 8 ounces of epoxy, but don't add any thickening powder. Pour it all out along the boat's keel. Quickly, before it runs onto the floor, start spreading it over the fiberglass. Bill likes to spread with a disposable bristle brush; he cuts off all but 1 inch of the bristles to make it stiffer for epoxy application. I prefer using a plastic spreader. With either tool, pull the epoxy down the hull, working from the center toward the edges to avoid wrinkling the cloth. Once you've contained the epoxy so it won't drip down the

Wet out the fiberglass with unthickened epoxy.

hull, try to move slowly so as not to mix air bubbles into the epoxy.

Mix and pour on more epoxy as needed, but use only the minimum amount required to saturate the cloth. Try not to *float* the cloth on a layer of epoxy by applying too much; the cloth must lie flat and in contact with the wood to achieve maximum strength. Check for the following problems as you *wet out* the cloth:

- If the surface appears bumpy or has washboardlike waves, it is floating. There is too much epoxy under the cloth. In this case, use your spreader or brush to squeeze out the excess epoxy. Try to pick up the epoxy with a brush and get it back into the mixing cup if you've poured on so much that you can't spread it to another area.

- Shiny spots are caused by too much epoxy on the surface of the cloth; brush the epoxy to a dry area. Again, pick up some epoxy with a brush if there are no more dry areas.

- White spots indicate too little epoxy; the cloth is not fully saturated. Pour a little more epoxy onto these areas and work it into the cloth.

- Pay attention to the seam between the #1 to #2 planks; the cloth won't lie quite flat here, and you'll need a little extra epoxy to cover it. This may cause the cloth to float at the edge, but it's hard to avoid.

The fiberglass should be smooth, dull, and transparent when it's properly saturated with epoxy. With all my warnings, this may seem a daunting step, but

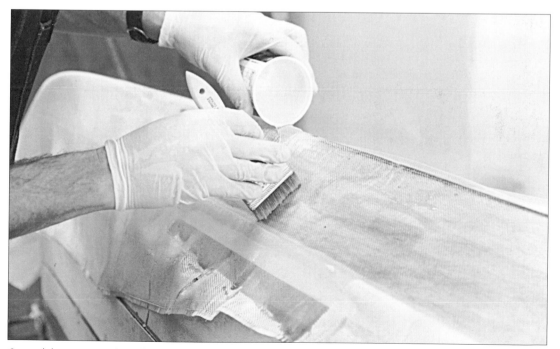

Spread the epoxy with a plastic squeegee or a disposable brush.

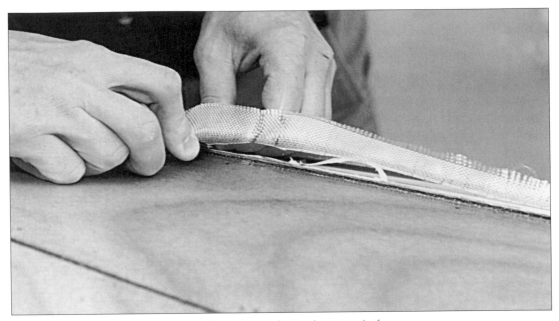

When the epoxy starts to harden, cut off the excess glass with a razor knife.

glassing is really not difficult as soon as you see what the result should look like. It's mostly a matter of brushing more epoxy onto those areas that need it and brushing epoxy off the areas that have too much. Take your time and be sure the cloth lies flat; sight down the bottom to check. A good glassing job saves sanding time later.

When the epoxy has started to harden and is no longer sticky, cut the cloth carefully along the masking tape, at the lower edge of the #2 plank, with a utility knife. Then pull off the excess.

Next we'll glass the stems to help hold the planks together and protect them from encounters with docks, logs, and other craft. Cut two strips of fiberglass cloth about 4 inches wide and 15 inches long. But cut these strips on a bias, or at a 45-degree angle to the weave, as shown in the photo.

Bias-cut cloth is stronger because more fibers cross the sharp stems. It's also easier to make bias-cut cloth conform to the shapes of the bow and stern. You can buy bias-cut fiberglass, but for small areas it's easier and cheaper to cut your own from a scrap piece of regular fiberglass. Place the bias-cut strips over the stems and pull and massage them so they conform to their shapes. The weave will shift and stretch to perfectly cover the area. The strips can hang down below the hull to be trimmed off after the epoxy cures. You'll wet out the cloth as you did on the hull bottom, but some builders prefer to brush a little epoxy onto the area first to help stick the strips into place. As you wet out this small piece of cloth, it may shift and wrinkle; simply smooth it out with your gloved hand.

If you paddle in rocky areas, you may want to add additional fiberglass on your canoe's bottom. You can simply put a second layer of fiberglass cloth over the first. Lay it right over the wet epoxy and wet it out just as you did the first layer. Of course, a second layer of fiberglass adds a few pounds to the boat—it's not just the weight of the glass, but also the weight of the extra epoxy required to saturate it. To save weight, I prefer to add extra glass only along the keel line, because that's where most abrasion occurs. Various widths of fiberglass tape, which is simply narrow cloth, are available in rolls or by the foot in both regular and bias cut. Of course, you can also cut your own tape from wider fiberglass cloth. I always apply a layer of 3-inch tape from stem to stem, and I add a second layer at the base of the stems. The tape should be laid right over the wet fiberglass cloth and saturated with epoxy. When the epoxy cures, you'll need to sand the edges of the tape to blend, or feather, them into the cloth.

TOP: *Cut two rectangles of fiberglass on the bias. These will be used on the stems.*
BOTTOM: *Bill glasses the stem.*

As soon as the epoxy on the stems and bottom is no longer sticky, you can roll or brush on a second thin coat of epoxy. This second and subsequent third coat will fill the "pattern" in the cloth, making a smooth surface for paint or varnish. I like to use a foam roller to apply the second coat because it's easier to apply a smooth, thin coat with a roller than with a brush. Again, try to avoid drips and runs. It's best to recoat the cloth soon after it hardens. If done within a couple of days, the epoxy forms a strong chemical bond. If it's more than 48 hours before you recoat, then lightly sand the surface to rough it up. Two to three coats of epoxy are usually required to fill the weave of the cloth, but more may be needed if they are very thin.

Many builders find that lightly sanding the cloth after the second coat results in a smoother finish and saves considerable sanding later. If you do this, though, be careful not to sand into the cloth. You'll see the fibers if you cut into the cloth, so stop sanding every few minutes to check that you've not gone too far down. Continue rolling on thin coats of epoxy until most of the pattern in the cloth has disappeared; a few areas of weave showing are OK, but most of the cloth should be smooth and shiny. Adding additional coats of epoxy once the weave is full won't increase strength, but it will add extra weight. The idea is to use as little epoxy as possible to do the job.

Glassing the Interior

Now we'll put some fiberglass on the inside of the hull, covering planks #1 and #2. Turn your canoe right side up and sand off any epoxy that's leaked through the seams or wire holes. Mask off the bottom edge of the #3 plank.

Make a small fillet along the keel line and between planks #1 and #2. Bill uses masking tape to keep the fillets straight and neat.

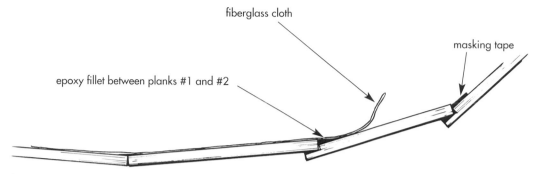

Glassing the inside of the hull.

Because fiberglass cloth won't conform to sharp edges, we must get rid of the small ridge between the #1 and #2 planks. Use your plane to knock down the step, then level it out with a tiny epoxy fillet. Also make a very small fillet, no more than ½ inch wide, to fill the keel seam. Use epoxy mixed with wood flour, just as you did on the fillets along the stems and bulkheads. Try to keep these fillets neat and even since you'll see them whenever you're in the boat. Bill masks these fillets with tape to keep them neat and pulls off any excess epoxy putty with the masking tape.

You can fiberglass right over the wet fillets as most boatbuilders do. But if you're a perfectionist, wait for them to

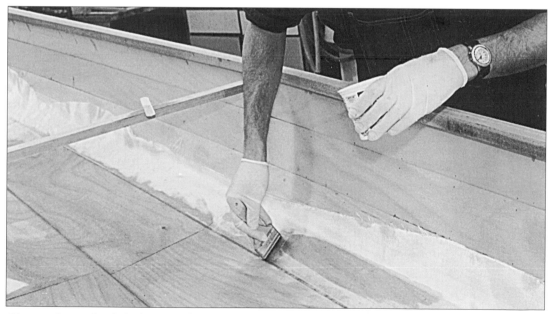

Glassing the inside of planks #1 and #2.

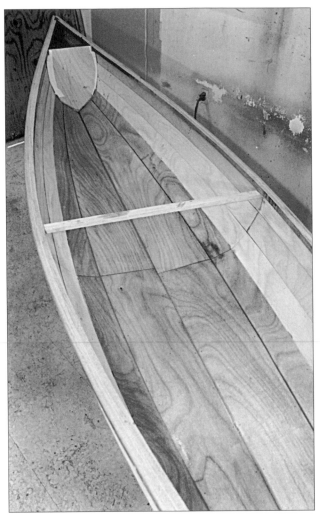

It's important to do a neat job of fiberglassing the inside of the hull.

harden, then sand them perfectly smooth and even.

Place the remaining length of fiberglass cloth over the #1 and #2 planks and trim it off just outside the masking tape. Also trim it even with the bulkhead fillets and check for sawdust and threads under the fiberglass.

Wet out the cloth as you did on the outside of the hull, working quickly and neatly. Be careful not to let excess epoxy pool along the keel. You'll probably varnish the inside of your canoe, so try to do a particularly neat job fiberglassing it. Spend some extra time pushing down any air bubbles and wetting out even the smallest dry spot. You'll find that it's harder to glass the inside of the hull, but once the epoxy is spread out, you'll have plenty of working time to get it perfect.

After the epoxy starts to harden, cut off the excess fiberglass at the edge of the #3 plank and peel up the masking tape. Sand the edge of the cloth so it blends with the wood. You can brush on more epoxy until the cloth's weave disappears as you did on the outside, or you might prefer to leave the texture of the fiberglass for better footing.

CHAPTER NINE

▶*Fitting Out*

With the hull completed, we turn our efforts to installing the decks, thwart, and seats. If you're an experienced woodworker, this may be the time to pull out those prized bits of exotic hardwood, show off your skills by making an inlay on the decks, or carve a fancy thwart.

Installing the Decks

The decks form the tops of the flotation compartments. Some builders fill this space with foam. But I prefer to leave them empty, since air is the best, and lightest, flotation of all, so long as the compartments remain sealed. Bill often installs plastic watertight inspection ports in the bulkheads. These are made for larger fiberglass craft and are available in any marine store. They allow cameras, wallets, and other nonwaterproof valuables to be stored in the flotation chambers.

Before installing the decks, coat all the interior surfaces of the flotation compartments with two coats of unthickened epoxy; don't forget the underside of the inwales. Also coat the underside of the deck itself. This will seal the wood, preventing water and rot penetration, should water somehow find its way into the compartments.

You can cut the deck from the same plywood as the hull, but many builders prefer to use a contrasting wood. Because the decks are well sealed and flat, furniture-grade walnut, cherry, Honduran mahogany, or other attractive plywood or solid wood can be used.

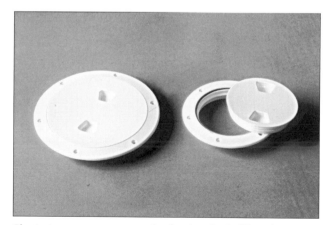

Plastic inspection ports may be fitted in the bulkheads to provide dry storage for small items. They are available in several sizes from marine supply stores.

The deck should cover the top edge of plank #5, but it should not extend onto the outwales. There is a pattern for the deck in the plans, but as each canoe will vary slightly in shape, I prefer to trace the deck's shape directly from the boat. To do this, place the blank from which the deck will be cut in position and trace the outside edge of the outwales onto its underside. The deck's edge is ¾ inch inside the traced line, since that's the width of the outwales, so draw a line that's ¾ inch in from the one you just traced. It's wise to cut the deck out a little proud of the inside line and then plane the edges for a perfect fit. The exact shape of curve at the deck's back edge is not critical, but it should be even and attractive, and extend about an inch past the bulkhead. An easy way to draw this curve is by tracing part of a large circle, such as a trash can lid, or bend a batten to a pleasing curve.

Adding the deck to the canoe is a good place to show off your woodworking skills. You might try making the deck from strips of solid wood instead of plywood; use up some of those scraps of zebrawood or rosewood cluttering your shop. Or make an inlaid or burned design on the decks. Bill made nice decks for one of his boats from ⅜-inch-thick Honduran mahogany to match the outwales. When using solid wood, taper and round over the outside edges to make the deck appear thinner than it really is; the entire canoe will look lighter and more elegant as a result. The nicest-looking decks fit between the inwales, rather than over them, as shown on the plans, but they are much harder to fit. If you do this, the bevel at

Clamping the deck.

the ends of the inwales must be perfect, and there's a lot of planing and fitting involved. Look through some of the books on canoe building listed in appendix 2 for more ideas on deck and trim options.

Clamping the deck into place can be tricky. The arrangement of sticks shown in the photo is the method Bill uses. I often tack the deck down with two brass brads, so it won't slip while being clamped. Glue the deck down with epoxy thickened with silica. After the deck is in place, make a fillet at the deck-to-bulkhead joints to ensure that the flotation compartments are airtight.

The splash guards at the inside edges of the decks are important because they reinforce the deck and make a convenient handhold for lifting the canoe. The easiest way to make them is to cut them from solid wood and round the top edges. Taper their ends to give a slimmer appearance, as shown in the photo below. Glue the splash guards to the aft edge of the decks. A skilled woodworker might enjoy laminating the splash guards from thin strips of solid wood glued to the back edge of the deck.

Making and Installing the Thwart

You can buy ready-made thwarts in various lengths in canoe shops or from some of the catalogs listed in appendix 2, but it's not difficult to cut your own. The thwart should be made from a very strong wood: most canoe builders use ash or white oak. The simplest thwart is a straight ¾- by

A simple splash guard cut from solid wood.

1½-inch stick. Round over the corners with a router or by sanding, and there you have it. I rather like these simple thwarts, but most paddlers seem to prefer one in the traditional double hourglass shape. To make a shaped thwart, start with a blank ¾ inch thick, about 2½ inches wide, and as long as your canoe is wide. Transfer the measurements shown in the plans to the blank. Or make up your own shape for the thwart. Cut out the thwart with a saber saw or bandsaw, sand it smooth, and round over the corners.

Other thwart options include substituting a portage yoke for the thwart or fitting an angled kneeling thwart for solo paddling. These are also available premade from canoe shops, or you can make your own. Of course, a portage yoke will require a lot of sanding and shaping if it's

to be comfortable, but if you make your own, it will be shaped exactly to your anatomy.

The thwart's length should be about ¼ inch shorter than the boat's beam at its eventual location. You'll position the thwart exactly amidships if building the Sassafras 16 with two seats. If building the Sassafras 12 or 14 with a center seat, place the thwart 9 inches behind the centerline. Slide a ⅛-inch shim (a thick piece of cardboard will do) between the end of the thwart and the hull. These shims will ensure that the thwart does not bear on, and deform, the hull planking. Secure the thwart to the inwale with two 1¼-inch stainless or bronze screws at each end. Drive the screws from the bottom so the heads don't show on top of the inwale. Be sure to predrill the holes. Don't glue in the

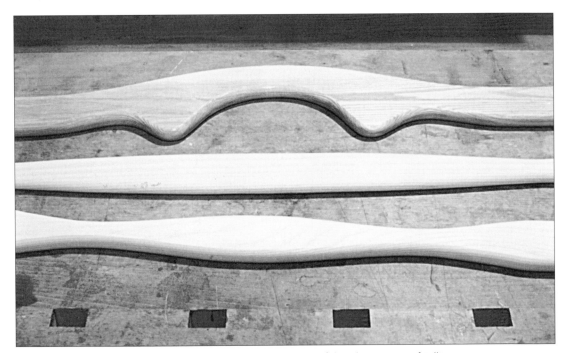

Commercially made portage yoke and thwart are at the top of the photo. One of Bill's thwarts is at the bottom.

ABOVE: *Fitting the thwart; this can be done after painting and varnishing, as Bill shows.* **RIGHT:** *Drive the screws from the bottom so the heads don't show.*

thwart; you'll want to remove it when painting or varnishing. Pull out the shims, leaving a small space between the end of the thwart and the hull.

Making the Seats

The easiest way to make seats is to pull out your credit card and order them. Nicely made and inexpensive cane and webbing canoe seats, as well as kayak seats that are adaptable to canoes, are available from a number of the suppliers listed in appendix 2. Still, some of us prefer to make our own, so here are directions for making

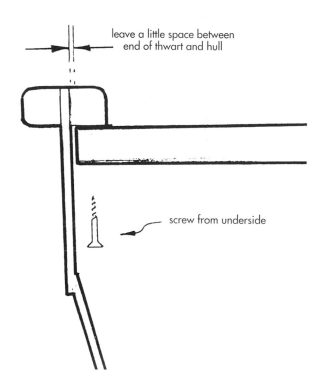

leave a little space between end of thwart and hull

screw from underside

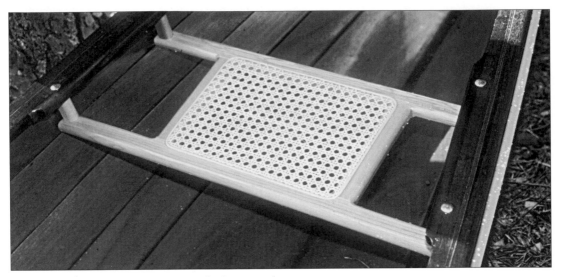

Commercially made cane canoe seats look nice and are inexpensive.

simple slat seats, web seats, and a kayak-style seat. Again, use a strong wood such as ash or white oak for canoe seats.

The slat-style seat is easy to make and comfortable enough for short trips, and, if you have a table saw, it can be made in less than an hour. Cut the two long pieces to span the hull and about ¾ inch thick and 1½ inch wide. Make the slats ½ inch wide, ⅜ inch thick, and 9 inches long. Attach the slats to the crosspieces with 1-inch #6 bronze wood screws and epoxy,

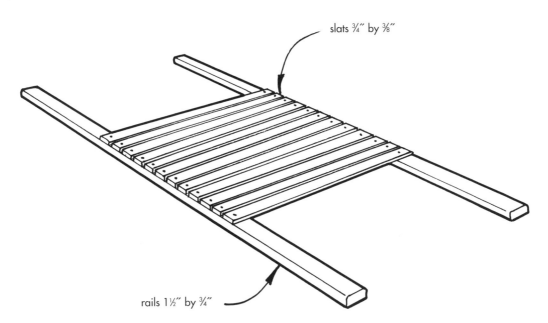

slats ¾″ by ⅜″

rails 1½″ by ¾″

A slat-style canoe seat.

leaving ¼-inch gaps between the slats. But sand and round over the corners of all the pieces before assembling them.

The web seat is more comfortable than the slat type and holds up better than the common caned canoe seats. But it's harder to make than the slat seat. The four frame pieces are ¾ by 1¼ inch and joined with a lap joint, as shown in the sketch on page 114. Cut the lap joint by making repeated cuts on a table saw, or cut the outside edges with a handsaw and chip out the joint with a chisel. Note that the lap faces up so it's compressed when you sit; this makes a much stronger seat than having the lap face down. The distance between the frame pieces is determined by the width of the webbing you choose and the space between webbing strips. The webbing should be Dacron or polyester, which is available in many colors and widths; don't buy nylon webbing because it fades from exposure to sunlight. Bill uses black 1-inch-wide webbing

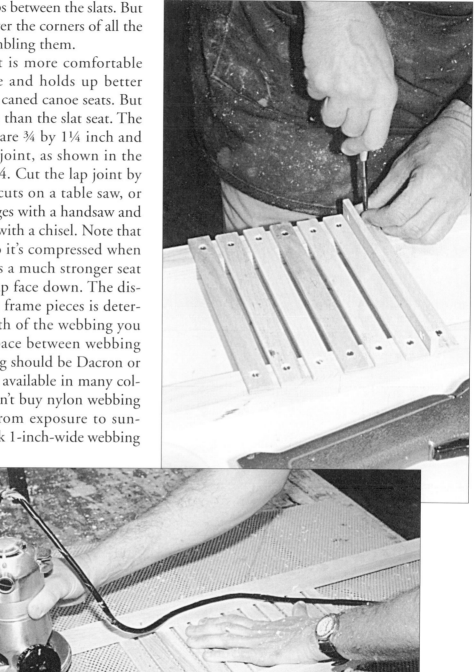

TOP: *A slat seat is easy to make. Use an extra slat to keep the spacing even, as shown here.*
BOTTOM: *Round over the seat frame for a more finished look.*

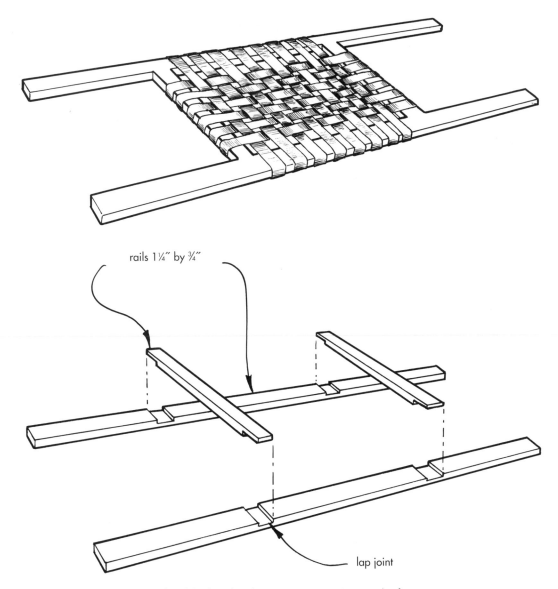

rails 1¼" by ¾"

lap joint

TOP: *The web seat is more comfortable than the slat seat.* **BOTTOM:** *Joining the frame pieces.*

and leaves a ¼-inch space in between. To make sure the webbing will be evenly spaced, lay out the webbing on the seat frame and mark the position of each strap with a pencil before cutting the lap joints. Predrill screw holes in the bottom of the frame at the proper spacing. Cut the webbing into strips of the required length and seal the ends over a flame. Attach one end of the strip to the underside of the frame with a ¾-inch #8 stainless or bronze wood screw and a finish washer. Wrap the strip around the frame piece and stretch it over the top to the opposite frame piece. Attaching the other end is tricky because the webbing must be stretched tight. You

ABOVE: *The frame for the web seat is made using lap joints.* RIGHT: *Bill is using an awl, just visible in his palm, to tighten the seat webbing.*

can pull the end of the webbing tight with pliers, but Bill's easier method is to push an awl through the webbing and use it as a lever against the frame to pull the webbing, then drive the second screw. Attach all the webbing this way, weaving it under and over the cross strips. One last thing about web seats: you might want to varnish the frame before attaching the webbing.

One nice-looking and comfortable variation of the web seat uses heavy canvas that is stretched over the frame and secured either by screws or by a line running through grommets set in the edge of the canvas. The edges must be folded over or hemmed and sewn, a task that I, for one,

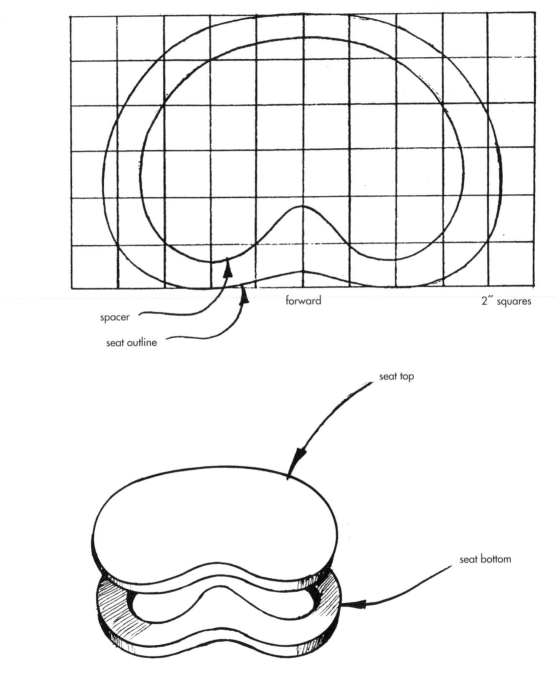

spacer

seat outline

forward

2″ squares

seat top

seat bottom

This simple but comfortable seat can be made from Minicel foam.

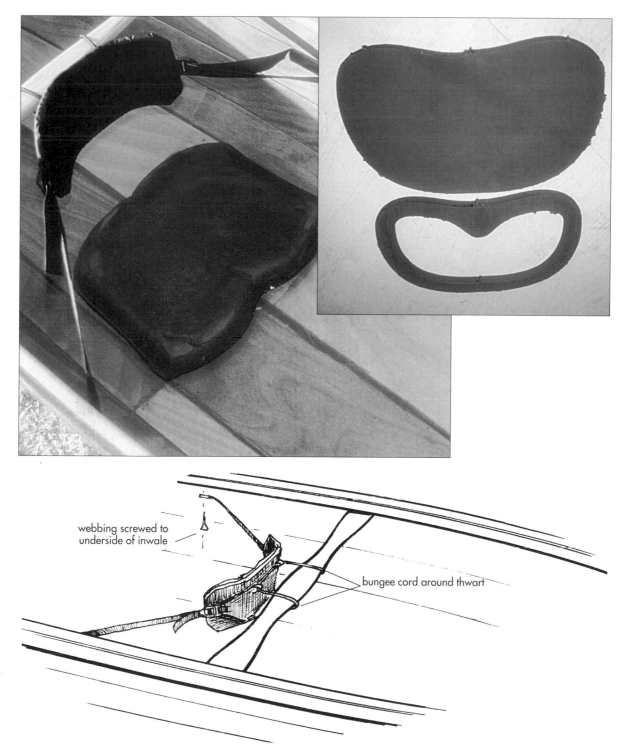

TOP LEFT: *A kayak-type seat installed in a Sassafras 12.* **TOP RIGHT:***Parts for the foam kayak-style seat can be cut with a saw or razor knife.* **BOTTOM:** *Rigging a kayak-style backband in a canoe.*

webbing screwed to
underside of inwale

bungee cord around thwart

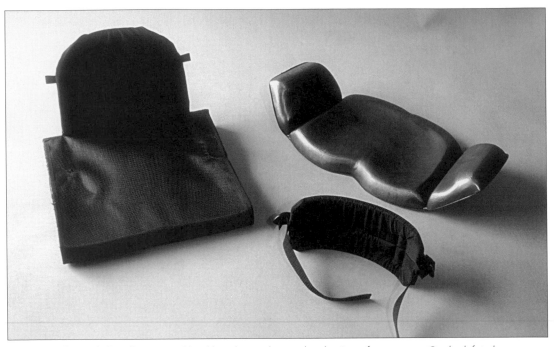

Commercially made kayak seats and backbands may be used in the Sassafras canoes. On the left is the Creature Comfort seat, to the right is the Happy Bottom Pad, and a Rapid Pulse backband rests below.

seem incapable of performing neatly.

If you're building a solo canoe and plan to use a double, or kayak, paddle, I suggest installing a kayak-style seat. The seat shown in the sketches on page 116 is easy to make from two layers of ¾-inch foam and is surprisingly comfortable. Be sure to use a high-quality closed-cell foam intended for seats or boat cushions. To make the seat, cut out the two layers and glue them together. The best glue for foam seats is automotive weather-stripping cement, which is available at any auto-parts store.

Installing the Seats

To install canoe seats, first determine their position(s). Suggested placement is shown on the plans, but an experienced canoeist might want to vary the position.

A solo seat should be positioned so the front edge of the paddler's bottom is over the center point of the boat. With two paddlers of equal weight, the distance from the center of the boat to the front edge of the bow seat should equal the distance from the center of the boat to the front edge of the stern seat. If, however, the paddlers are of vastly different weights, you can calculate the relative positions. Multiply the distance from the center of the boat to the front edge of the bow seat by the weight of the bow paddler. This should equal the weight of the stern paddler multiplied by the distance from the center of the boat to the front edge of stern seat.

Canoe seats are hung from the in-wales with long bolts. Spacers made from

Seat-installation kits are available at many canoe shops.

dowels with a hole drilled through their centers, or rectangular blocks with a slot cut into their back faces, cover the bolts. Before you run all over town looking for the proper ¼-inch bronze or stainless steel bolts, washers, and nuts, let me tell you that canoe seat hardware kits are readily available. They contain not only the hardware but also premade ash spacers that you need only cut to length.

You can make your own seat hangers by drilling through a dowel or by sanding the corners off a square section, then drilling it.

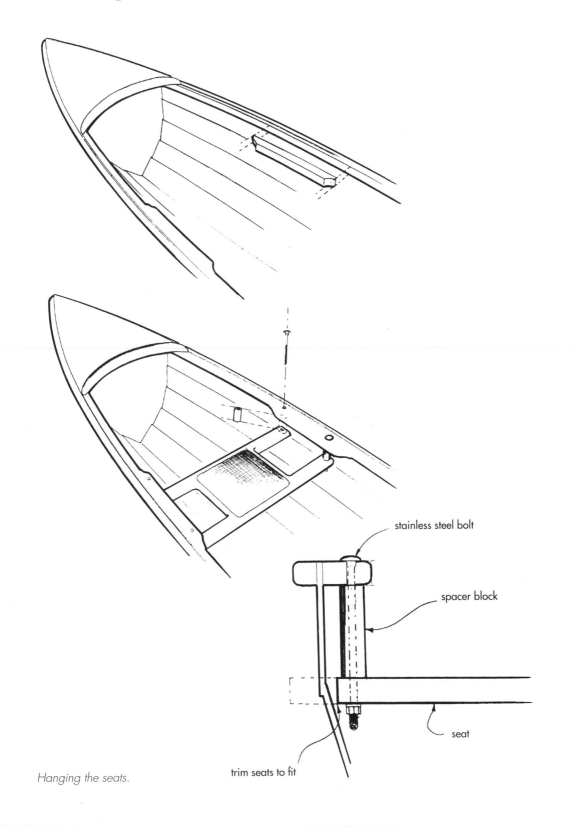

stainless steel bolt

spacer block

seat

trim seats to fit

Hanging the seats.

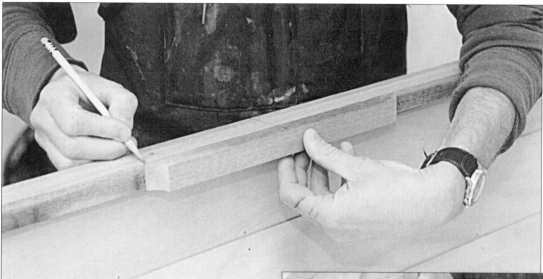

ABOVE: *Scribe the seat doublers, then plane them to fit.* RIGHT: *Glue the doubler to the inside of the in wale.* BOTTOM: *The finished doubler.*

The inwales in our canoes are a little too narrow to drill for a bolt. So before we install the seats, we'll increase the width of the inwale above the seats by gluing on a *doubler*. The doubler is nothing more than a leftover piece of inwale stock a few inches longer than the seat is wide. I like to cut an ogee or other decorative shape at the ends of the doublers before gluing them in. Hold the doubler beside the inwale and trace the inwale's curve onto its top. Using your sander or plane, shape the back of the doubler to the curve of the inwale. The curve is very slight, so this only takes a few minutes, but it prevents the doubler from causing an unsightly flat spot on the gunwale. Glue the doublers into place with epoxy thickened with silica.

Trim the seat's frame to fit in the desired location, and drill holes for the bolts

in the gunwale and in the seat itself. The centers of the holes should be on the glue line between the doubler and the inwale. It's easiest to have an assistant hold the seat directly under the inwale while you drill the hole through both.

The height of the seats is a matter of personal preference; I like the seats on the Sassafras 16 about the same height as the top of the #4 plank. For the Sassafras 14, start with the seat about ½ inch below the top of the #4 plank. After a test paddle, you can adjust the height; remember that lowering the seats even ½ inch will dramatically increase the stability of the canoe. When you are satisfied with the height of the seats, cut the spacers to the

TOP: *The seats should be level.* **BOTTOM:** *Bill tests his new seat; notice his innovative level/paddle.*

proper length and install them over the bolts. You might also like to cut off any excess from the bolts with a hacksaw so they don't protrude beyond the nut.

Installing commercially made kayak-type seats is simply a matter of gluing them to the bottom per the manufacturer's instructions, or leaving them loose. The cut foam seat described earlier can be glued down with contact cement or, better, automotive weather-stripping cement. The backband is secured to the inwales with screws and tied to the thwart as shown in the sketch on page 117. Don't install the seat and backband until you've varnished or painted the inside of your canoe.

Finishing the Gunwales

Before final sanding and varnishing, round over the corners of the inwales, outwales, and any other trim with sharp edges. You might have done this on the outwales before installing them; in any case, use a sander and block plane or a router with a round-over bit to make a smooth radius on

Round over the inwales and outwales with a router or with a plane and sandpaper.

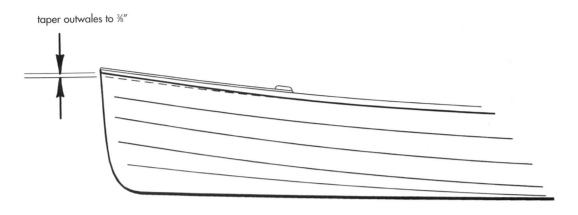

taper outwales to ⅜"

Taper the outwales for a more elegant look.

all the corners. I like to stop the radii on the inwales an inch or two from the decks and thwart; this adds a little complexity to the design and looks nice.

Another nice touch is to taper the ends of the outwales to give the boat a lighter, more elegant look. Use your plane to reduce the thickness of the outwales as they approach the canoe's ends. Start about 2 feet back and taper them to ⅜-inch thickness at the end.

CHAPTER TEN

▸*Painting and Varnishing*

A little paint, a little varnish, and your canoe will be finished; if only life were so simple. First we must face that boatbuilder's nemesis: sanding—not just a few hours of sanding, but a whole day of sawdust, boredom, and sore arms. Then we'll fight dust, bubbles, drips, kamikaze insects, runs, and sags, in trying to achieve a yachtlike finish. It won't be fun, and you may curse me for getting you into this, but eventually you'll look at your gleaming masterpiece, and it'll all be worth it.

Epoxy Saturation

Before sanding, varnishing, and painting, I like to coat the entire boat, inside and out, with two coats of unthickened epoxy. The epoxy soaks into the wood, filling and reinforcing the grain, particularly the grain opened by bending. It adds a tough outer skin that increases the abrasion resistance and the strength of the hull, and it provides a smooth clear base that adds depth to a varnish finish. Epoxy also makes an ideal base for paint or varnish.

These finishes usually fail when water finds its way into the wood and causes the paint or varnish to blister or lift. But epoxy bonds to the wood, making a waterproof shell that prevents water from undermining the finish.

On the other hand, epoxy is much harder to sand and, as you know by now, it doesn't flow or level well, so applying a smooth coat is difficult. If you'll be gentle with your new creation, keep it stored in a warm, dry place, and fix any scratches as soon as they appear, you can dispense with epoxy saturation. After all, the bottom is already fiberglassed.

If you do choose to epoxy coat the entire hull, start by vacuuming or brushing off any sawdust on or in the boat. The best tool for applying epoxy over large areas is a foam roller. Roll a thin layer of epoxy over the entire surface; most of this first coat will be absorbed into the wood. Rollers tend to leave small bubbles on the epoxy's surface. *Tip off* the epoxy by running a disposable brush over the fresh epoxy to pop these bubbles; just skim the surface lightly with the brush. Brush any areas you couldn't reach with the roller. Also brush out any runs or drips to save sanding them out later. When the epoxy has hardened, sand lightly, and then roll on the second coat and again brush out any bubbles and runs.

Try to apply the sealing coat of epoxy when air temperature is steady or falling. If you apply the coat early on a cool morning, rising air temperature will cause the air in the wood to expand and escape through the wet epoxy. This is called *outgassing*; it forms thousands of tiny bubbles in the epoxy, which you'll have to sand smooth.

When the last coat of epoxy has cured, wash the boat with detergent and water to remove any amine blush left by the curing epoxy. Amine blush is that waxy film that clogs sandpaper and prevents paint and varnish from drying. Two thorough washes with a scrub pad and warm soapy water, followed by a rinse, will remove it. Sanding won't remove amine blush; it would be like trying to sand butter off toast. If you used an epoxy that's resistant to blushing, such as MAS with slow hardener, you can skip this step.

Sanding

Let me say right at the onset that I absolutely loathe sanding, which is one reason why I'm the boat designer and you're the builder. This attitude may come through in my writing, but don't let it put you off—even though you'll most likely awaken on sanding day with a dreading heart and shuffle to the shop like a condemned prisoner. At least you can make sanding bearable by wearing a good-quality mask or respirator that stops dust yet provides plenty of air. If using an elec-

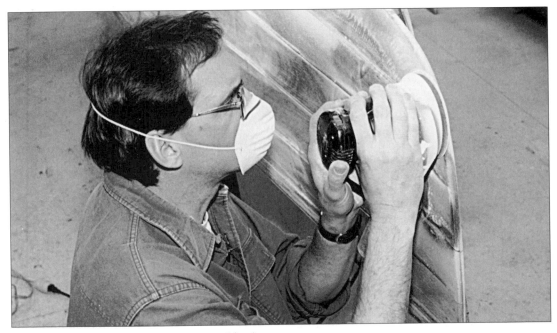

Sanding, and lots of it, is the key to a good finish.

tric sander, get a set of earplugs. And stock up on sandpaper so you're not sanding with dull sheets. Finally, if it's a nice breezy day, move your canoe outside for sanding—and stand upwind.

Start with 80-grit paper on your sanding block and random-orbital sander. The electric sander will work well on the outside of the hull and make the work go fast, but the sander won't fit on the planks inside, so this is where you'll spend hours hand sanding.

There is some technique to this sanding business. Hold the sanding pad flat against the hull; pressing down the edge of the spinning disc or pad will make grooves that are almost impossible to smooth out. Work steadily from one end of the boat to the other. Change paper often, at least every 2 to 3 feet; fresh sandpaper cuts much faster and leaves fewer marks. Sandpaper is expensive, which is why you bought boxes of 25 or 50 sheets instead of those overpriced little sleeves from the home-improvement store. Don't make things harder by using worn-out paper.

The plank overlaps may present a problem because the sander won't work in the narrow corners, but a file turned on edge does a good job of cleaning them up, or use sandpaper wrapped around a wooden block. When you've finished sanding an epoxied area, the entire surface should be an even, dull white; don't worry, it'll become clear again under varnish. Shiny spots indicate a low or unsanded area that needs more work. If you accidentally sand through the epoxy layer, and you will, recoat the area and sand it again later.

There will eventually come a time when you think you're done. That means that it's time to sand the whole boat again, this time with 120-grit and then 220-grit sandpaper to eliminate swirls and sanding marks. But this won't take nearly as long as the initial sanding. If you plan to paint the hull and use a high-build primer under the paint, you can stop sanding it after the 80-grit.

A few masochistic builders like to roll on several more coats of epoxy after the initial sanding to build up a deep, glasslike base for the varnish. These subsequent coats must be sanded, too. I admit that even I have done this on a few boats. The finish is indeed impressive, but adding more epoxy coats sure was a lot of extra mind-numbing work, and it added a lot of extra weight to the boat.

After sanding, wash your canoe again to remove all traces of sanding dust. Epoxy dust is tenacious stuff that won't just rinse off with a casual spray. You'll need to go over the boat several times with a damp towel or sponge.

Fairing Putty and Primer

If you are planning to varnish your canoe, fairing putties and primers are not an option, but they can greatly improve a paint job. With the final sanding completed, take a well-deserved break, then examine the entire surface of your boat inch by inch and circle every imperfection with a soft pencil. You'll be surprised at how many you find. Fill low spots with acrylic putty or with a fairing putty made by mixing epoxy with a lightweight, easily sanded thickener such as microballoons or Microlight. You can use wood flour with epoxy for fairing instead, but it's harder to sand. Acrylic putty is available at all auto-parts stores, but the automotive type is red. Marine stores carry white putty that's easier to cover with light-colored paint. Acrylic putty is a fast-drying paste that sands easily. It does shrink when drying and so is only suitable for use in shallow imperfections.

Primer is a thick, easily sanded paint that fills even the tiniest imperfections in the hull, leaving a perfectly smooth surface for the paint. If a yacht-quality paint job is your goal, a high-build primer under the paint will make it far easier to achieve. On the other hand, primer is softer than most paints and makes the hull more easily scratched. It also adds another round of sanding. Some high-build primers use talc as filler, while others use microballoons. The microballoon type is more durable.

If you decide to prime, brush and roll on two coats of the stuff and allow it to dry. Don't worry if the primer coat isn't smooth: you'll sand off most of what you've applied. Sanding high-build primer generates copious quantities of baby powder–like dust; sand it outside. You'll be pleasantly surprised at how quickly you'll have a hull as smooth as the proverbial baby's bottom. Now sand with 80-, then 120-, and finally 220-grit sandpaper.

Paints and Varnishes

Most novice boatbuilders love varnish and want every square inch of their boat *bright* (that's what boatbuilders call varnished wood). But there's a lot to be said for paint. It holds up better than varnish, and it is more abrasion resistant and easier to touch up. Fewer coats of paint are required, and you can use fairing compound and high-build primer under the paint to achieve a smoother, more efficient, and faster finish. Even larger scratches or chips in the wood can be repaired with thickened epoxy and hidden under paint.

But surface irregularities and poor sanding are actually more visible on a painted surface than on a varnished one. I think this is because people are a little awestruck by shiny expanses of varnished wood, and they don't notice the surface details under it. Also, the pattern of the grain acts like camouflage, hiding shapes and details. Bill says that it's easier to sell a boat with lousy varnish than one with perfect paint. But despite paint's drawbacks, both Bill and I think that a light-color paint really shows off the shape of those beautiful planks you spent so much time and effort cutting, assembling, and sanding.

So my advice is to paint the outside of your canoe and varnish the inside; that's the only way I'd finish a lapstrake boat. And I'd use only white, crème, or light blue or light green paint so I could see the lovely shadows cast by the overlap of the planks. By the way, you must apply some sort of finish to your boat; epoxy deteriorates in sunlight, turning milky and dull. It must be protected from ultraviolet (UV) radiation with either paint or marine varnish.

You'll certainly want to varnish at least part of your canoe, even if only the gunwales and decks, and it's important to use the right varnish. Marine varnishes have UV filters that allow them to stand up to sunlight longer than other types, and UV radiation is the reason that varnish, as well as epoxy, eventually breaks down. Stick to established marine brands such as Z-Spar, Epifanes, and Interlux. Applying a fine varnish finish is hard enough, so don't make it tougher by using inferior household varnish or a one-part polyurethane. So-called spar varnishes sold at home-improvement and hardware stores are not acceptable. Nor are one-part marine polyurethane varnishes, tung oil furniture finishes, or various concoctions intended for use on the exterior teak of your big boat.

Each of the marine finish manufacturers makes several types of varnish. There are subtle differences between the types and brands. Much of varnishing involves getting a feel for the varnish you're using, so don't change brands or types once you've gotten the hang of it. We used Z-Spar's Captain's Varnish exclusively at Chesapeake Light Craft. I know that Z-Spar makes a high-end varnish called Flagship that's supposed to hold up better. But we found it was harder to apply than Captain's Varnish, so we stuck with Captain's for eight years.

Two-part polyurethane marine varnishes are another option. These are very hard and abrasion-resistant clear finishes; they stand up to sunlight well and are compatible with epoxy. Despite these advantages, many builders still prefer traditional oil-based varnishes. I've tried two-part polyurethanes, but I'm not fond of them because they're very expensive, harder to apply than oil-based varnish, and lack the golden color oil-based var-

It's easiest to varnish seat frames and thwarts by hanging them so you can reach all sides.

nishes imparts on mahogany. Two-part polyurethanes are essentially clear paints; so if you choose to use them, follow the instructions for applying two-part polyurethane paint.

I should mention that water-based varnishes are getting better all the time, but I haven't found one that is even close to the performance of traditional oil-based varnish. The types I've experimented with are not as transparent, don't hold up as well, and lack the gold tone of real varnish.

There are also many options in choosing paint, but most builders will use marine enamel, one-part polyurethane (good in paint, bad in varnish), or two-part polyurethane. Marine enamels are traditional oil-based paints. They give a fairly hard finish that's slightly flat, rather than glossy. Enamels are not expensive, as marine paints go, they are available in many colors, and they are easy to apply. On the down side, some types don't dry well over epoxy, and they are softer than polyurethane paints. Both Bill and I like the slightly old-fashioned soft look of these paints; after all, this is a wooden canoe, not a new Lexus.

Those boatbuilders who want gloss, and plenty of it, may prefer a one-part polyurethane such as Interlux's popular Brightside paint. These finishes are almost as glossy and durable as the paint on your car but far easier to apply. They are also available in a wide range of colors from several manufacturers. If you carefully apply them with a foam roller, most people will assume that a professional sprayed your finish.

If one-part polyurethane is still not shiny enough, two-part polyurethane is even harder and glossier. In fact, fiberglass boat manufacturers have been known to paint their show boats with it because it's so much glossier than gelcoat. Unfortunately, two-part polyurethane is also far more expensive and far more difficult to apply. The extreme gloss and relative thinness of these paints bring out every flaw in the underlying surface, so you must prepare your hull with fanatical care. If you do decide to try a two-part polyurethane, be sure to also buy the special thinner that's required to bring it to a brushing consistency.

There are other types of paint on the market, and new ones are being introduced each year. There are industrial latex paints intended for outdoor machinery and other metal surfaces that are as easy to apply but more durable than house paint. I tried one of these on the interior of my rowboat a few years ago, and it has held up remarkably well. A professional paint shop will carry such products and explain how to apply them.

In choosing the color of your paint, consider whether you'll be able to get more of it when you need to touch up a scrape. White paint is always available, while some less-popular colors are manufactured only once or twice a year, so if you run out, you might not find more for months.

You may need to thin any paint or varnish slightly if working on a hot day, but never by more than 10 percent. Buy the thinner recommended by the manufacturer. I know that you suspect that you're paying $15 for a few ounces of mineral spirits, but the recommended thinners always seem to work better. Varnishing just the inside of a canoe will require about a quart of varnish; the inside and outside will use up most of two. For painting the hull, you'll use close to a quart of paint and, if you choose to use it, a full quart of primer.

If you run into problems with a marine paint, don't hesitate to call the manufacturer. Marine paint companies have technical representatives who spend much of their time visiting boat shops and marinas and have seen just about every problem you can imagine. And they'll be happy to discuss or troubleshoot the application of their various products with you.

Tools for Finishing

The days of expensive badger bristle brushes are numbered. Disposable foam brushes and rollers do as good a job of laying on paint and varnish as a $30 brush. And you don't have to clean them in environmentally harmful solvents. Get 2-inch foam brushes, the sort with wooden, not plastic, handles—they seem to last longer. You'll also need some foam rollers. Find the type made for use with lacquer or epoxy; these are usually yellow with a 1/8-inch nap. Cut 7- or 9-inch rollers down to 3 inches and use them on narrow roller frames. Do not buy the black general-purpose foam rollers that disintegrate when used with epoxy. In my experience, these brushes and rollers are available at some paint stores and all marine stores but not at home-improvement centers.

If you're experienced with a spray gun, you may be tempted to spray your finish. But don't assume that you'll get a better finish. Bill is a very competent sprayer who applies flawless lacquer finishes to huge pieces of custom furniture he builds. Yet he admits that a brush can lay down just as smooth a coat. He also says that the skill level required is about the same with either method. Bill often brushes on a coat of varnish rather than take the time to set up, and later clean, his spray gun. Most folks who see his work assume that all his finishes are sprayed. If you do decide to spray, contact the paint manufacturer for specific instructions.

Some marine finishes, particularly two-part polyurethane, are very toxic when atomized, so a positive-pressure respirator must be worn while spraying them; I'm not exaggerating—people have died spraying this stuff.

If applying both paint and varnish to the same boat, you'll need to mask off the varnished area, then the painted surface, or vice versa. Marine finishes are thin and will bleed under regular paper masking tape, leaving a ragged edge. This is not a problem if the paint/varnish line is hidden under the gunwale, but visible delineations should be masked only with plastic 3M Fine Line tape that's available at auto-parts, paint, and marine stores. The trick to getting a clean delineation between paint and varnish is to press the edge of the tape down firmly so paint can't seep under it. Don't leave paper masking tape in place for more than a few hours or plastic tape on for more than a couple days, or it may you take a couple more days to remove it.

Applying Varnish and Paint

The single most important step you can take toward ensuring a nice paint and varnish finish is to work in a dust-free area. Woodworking being anything but dust-free, the best solution is to find a room other than your shop in which to paint and varnish. If you must varnish in your shop, wet down the floor to settle dust stirred up by walking, vacuum the room, and keep the doors and windows closed to minimize air movement after you've finished.

Also, change out of the clothes you wore when sanding, and rinse the dust out of your hair and off your arms. There's more than one perfectionist out there who varnishes naked. Finally, remove the seats so they are not in the way.

If you see tiny "bubbles" in your dry varnish, they are dust particles. Yes, I know they look like bubbles, but they are dust. All you can do is try to vacuum again and keep the dust down when applying the next coat. Unless you have a special paint room or clean room, there will be some dust in your finish. As it says on the paint can: preparation really is 90 percent of a good finish job.

Before applying paint or varnish, read the directions on the can. No one knows more about the paint or varnish than its manufacturer, and advice is free and right there in front of you. Most paint manufacturers also give out free literature full of tips on applying their products; Interlux even includes a how-to audiotape with one of its paints.

Varnish and paint are sensitive to temperature and humidity; try to apply them only on warm, dry days. If you're working outdoors, plan to end early enough so the finish is almost dry before dew starts to form in the evening. Avoid painting or varnishing outdoors on very hot days, on cold days, in direct sunlight, on windy days, or when there are lots of bugs around. Lastly, if there's any chance it might rain, don't varnish outdoors; if it's already raining, don't even varnish indoors.

Never ever shake varnish, and don't use it directly out of the can; instead, pour as much as you'll need for one coat into a clean paper cup or can. And when you finish, don't even think of pouring the oxidized, dust-ridden remainder back into the can. If you'll be using a foam roller, pour the paint or varnish into a clean roller tray.

Applying a flawless coat of varnish is not technically difficult, but you must know how to do it. The best way to learn is by watching a skilled finisher. I know that may be difficult, so I'll try to describe Bill's method here. Dip just the tip of a 2-inch foam brush into the varnish; don't overload it. If you must wipe off excess varnish on the edge of the container, you've overloaded the brush. Brush on the varnish against the grain. If working on a foredeck, for example, start at the tip and make six or eight passes across the deck, working aft. Use slow, deliberate brush strokes. Dip the brush when it runs dry, but try to keep the coat as thin as possible. With an almost dry brush, brush the varnish again in the direction of the grain. Only brush in one direction, toward the starting point. Continue laying on varnish across the grain, just overlapping the completed area, then brush it with the grain again, ending each brush stroke in the wet area you just finished. If you look back at your work and see a few dry spots, don't be concerned; you'll repair them on the next coat. But runs indicate that the coat is too thick and will need to be sanded out. Don't stop varnishing until the coat is finished; you must always varnish into a *wet edge*, as the pros say. Learning to brush paint and varnish takes practice and a little talent. Don't be disappointed if the first coat is less than perfect. By the fourth or fifth coat, you'll be an expert.

When using foam brushes to apply varnish, lay the varnish on across the grain, then smooth it out in the direction of the grain. And never use varnish straight from the can.

That's right, a good varnish job requires four or more coats. It's best to wait two days after applying the first coat of varnish to recoat, and then overnight between subsequent coats. Hand sand lightly between coats with 400-grit wet/dry sandpaper or with a fine 3M sanding pad. In case you're not familiar with wet/dry sandpaper, use it on a rubber sanding block just as you would ordinary sandpaper, but dip the block and paper into a bucket of water every few minutes. The water washes away the dust that would otherwise quickly clog such fine sandpaper. Remember that your aim is to dull and smooth the surface, not to re-

Sand with 400-grit paper or with a fine-grit sanding pad between coats.

move all the finish you so tediously applied the day before. Sanding the surface should take only a few minutes. Wipe off the sanding dust with wet paper towels and then with a tack cloth. You'll need at least four coats of varnish for a good finish, six or seven for a yacht-quality finish, and 12 to win a ribbon at the Wooden Boat Show.

You could apply paint with a brush, just as you did the varnish, but for the outside of the hull I recommend applying paint with a short-nap foam roller, then tipping it out with a brush. This technique works well for varnish, too, if the varnish is thinned a little. When using a roller, don't overload it with paint or varnish. Try to lay on a thin, even coat over about 1 square foot of the surface. Immediately put down the roller, pick up your brush, and gently run it over the surface to pop bubbles left by the roller and to smooth any runs. The brush should just

TOP: *Apply paint with a short-nap foam roller.* BOTTOM: *Tip the paint with a foam brush to pop bubbles left by the roller and to smooth the surface.*

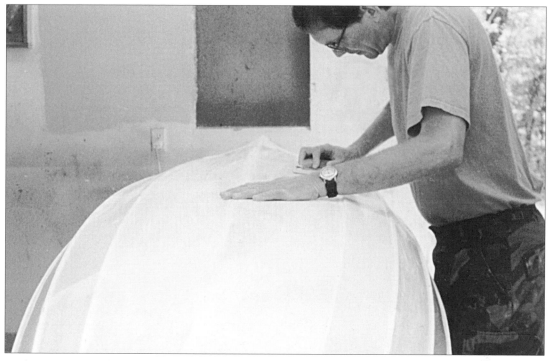

With 400-grit wet/dry sandpaper, lightly sand between coats of paint to level and dull the surface.

When the paint is dry, reinstall the seats.

It's finally time to load up and go paddling.

skim the paint. It's easier to have an assistant tip the paint as you continue to apply it. Paint sets up quickly, so you'll need to work fast. Try to always roll into a wet edge rather than into paint or varnish that has started to set.

Marine paints are thin, and you'll probably need at least three coats, but some colors, yellow in particular, require five or six. Wet-sand in between coats with 400-grit paper.

Again, as when varnishing, don't be discouraged if your first coat of paint isn't perfect. Sand it smooth and start over on the next coat. By the fourth or fifth coat, you'll get the hang of it.

Bill's new canoe.

Appendices

More Boat Designs

Many paddlers find that they enjoy building boats as much as using them. If you have fun building a Sassafras canoe, then you might also like some of my other designs. And once you've completed your Sassafras, you'll have the skill to build any of the boats described here, because they're all assembled stitch-and-glue style (though not all are LapStitch). Many of the boats I've drawn are kayaks, but I've also designed a sailboat, some pulling boats, and even a little trimaran. Plans for some of these boats are in my other books, *The Kayak Shop* (now out of print, but you may find it in used bookstores) and *The New Kayak Shop*, both published by Ragged Mountain Press. Full-size plans for all my designs and, in many cases, precut kits are available from Chesapeake Light Craft.

MILL CREEK

Thirty years ago, boats like the Mill Creeks would have been called double-

The stable Mill Creek double-paddle canoes (or are they kayaks?) are ideal for fishing, photography, or birding.

You can even sail a Mill Creek.

paddle canoes or, perhaps, decked canoes. But today they are termed kayaks. Whatever you call them, the Mill Creek kayaks are wider, shorter, and more stable than typical sea kayaks, and they are more seaworthy than open canoes. They serve much the same purpose as the Sassafras canoes, but they are for paddlers who venture onto open water. The Mill Creeks are stable enough for nature photography, fly-fishing, and birding. Their large, open cockpits allow easy entry and exit, while the high coamings ensure a dry cockpit, even without a kayak-style sprayskirt—that's important if you carry a camera or binoculars on your lap. I've also designed

a sailing rig for all three Mill Creeks.

The Mill Creeks have simple five-panel, multi-chine hulls with 6 mm bottoms and 4 mm sides and decks. They have long waterlines for good performance and sufficient volume in the ends to handle steep waves; I've paddled the 13-footer in 25-knot winds and 3-foot seas.

The Mill Creek 13 has a 250-pound capacity and enough room for minimal camping gear. At just 13 feet long and 36 pounds, it's easy to carry down to the water and to cartop. This is my favorite kayak for fly-fishing, and at least one professional fly-fishing guide on Florida Bay paddles this model. In fact, I would go so far as to say that of all the kayaks and canoes I've drawn, I am most proud of this one. It is not the fastest, or the roomiest, or perhaps even the prettiest, but once in a while everything in a boat design comes together in perfect balance.

The 15-foot version is longer, narrower, and carries more gear. This is the version for the touring paddler or anyone who seeks a little more performance in an open-cockpit kayak. The maximum load is 350 pounds.

The Mill Creek 16.5 is a very versatile boat. In addition to being a wonderful boat for two, it is small enough to be used solo once in a while. And if you get tired of paddling, drop in a sliding-seat rowing unit; it rows better than some purpose-built rowing craft I've tried. You can also step the mast, mount the leeboard, and let the wind do all the work. Several builders have even installed electric outboard motors. It is a little small for long-distance touring, but if you pack light . . .

CHESAPEAKE KAYAKS

The Chesapeake designs are all-around sea kayaks. The standard versions are meant for long-distance touring, while the lower-volume Chesapeake LT series is better suited to day-paddling and weekend trips. I believe that it's very important to have a sea kayak fit its paddler. So I've drawn three sizes of each of the two versions; I've also designed a double (two-person) and a triple (three-person) version.

The Chesapeake 16 is designed for small- to medium-size paddlers, 100 to 170 pounds. At 15 feet, 8 inches by 23 inches, it is fast and stable enough for serious touring. The 17-footer has a beam of 24 inches and weighs 46 pounds. It is best for paddlers weighing between 160 and 220 pounds, and there's capacity for another 50 pounds of camping gear. If you're heavier, up to 270 pounds, you'll want to build the Chesapeake 18. This is one big boat: with a beam of 24½ inches and a

weight of about 45 pounds, it will carry a total burden of well over 300 pounds. Plans and building instructions for the Chesapeake 16 are in *The New Kayak Shop*.

The Chesapeake kayaks were an instant hit among touring paddlers, and my company was soon selling hundreds of sets of plans for them each year. But many paddlers, who rarely camped from their kayaks, asked for a lower-volume version for day-paddling and the occasional weekend trip. So I went back to the computer and designed the light touring, or LT, versions of the Chesapeake. The Chesapeake LTs have the same proven hull shape as the original version but are lower and have a flatter aft deck. This reduces volume and windage and makes them a little lighter. Many shorter paddlers and Inuit-paddle devotees prefer the lower deck height and resulting lower paddle position.

The Chesapeake 16 is a fine boat for rough-water touring or flatwater exploring.

The Chesapeake double is simply a two-person version of the popular Chesapeake design.

The Chesapeake 21 is a large double, or triple, that's perfect for couples who need to carry a lot of gear in a fast, stable sea kayak. Since its hull shape is based on the Chesapeake singles, it exhibits the same solid tracking, balance, and speed potential. In addition to the double shown in the photo, there is a three-cockpit version that's ideal for families with a child who is not yet old enough to paddle. It's also a good choice for those of you who simply must bring your pet along. Don't laugh; I've been asked about doggy sprayskirts. Before you decide to build a double or triple, you should be sure that you'll always have someone to go paddling with; these boats are simply too big to use as singles.

NORTH BAY AND NORTH BAY XL KAYAKS

The North Bay is my interpretation of the classic West Greenland kayaks. Many paddlers feel that West Greenland kayaks represented the highest form of kayak development. Indeed, it is difficult to argue with several thousand years of design evolution. I drew this design after studying numerous historical drawings of native skin boats.

With a narrow hard-chine hull, the North Bay tracks like a train and is almost as fast. A flat aft deck and high ends make Eskimo rolling easier. And you must appreciate that knowing how to roll is crucial given the North Bay's 20-inch beam. The boat's high-volume bow and stern and flared hull ensure great rough-water handling. There isn't much room in this boat, and I would recommend it only for day-paddling and only for the expert. The standard cockpit is very small, in keeping with traditional design, though it could easily be enlarged.

The North Bay XL is a wider version of the same boat. It is virtually identical save for the 2 inches of extra beam and the larger cockpit. I designed this version for the many folks who could not comfortably fit into the original. The additional stability resulting from the extra beam

ABOVE: *The North Bay is based on ancient West Greenland designs. It's fast, seaworthy, and demanding to paddle.* RIGHT: *The Patuxent designs are fast racing kayaks.*

makes this version suitable for athletic intermediate paddlers.

PATUXENT KAYAKS

The Patuxent 19.5 was designed as a homebuilt racing or training kayak. It turned out to be one of the fastest sea kayaks around, as proven by its continued success in races. Being so long, the boat requires a powerful paddler to take advantage of its speed potential. Less powerful and lighter paddlers may actually go faster (except during a sprint) in a shorter boat with less wetted-surface area. It is only 21 inches wide, so you should exercise caution in rough conditions; I capsized this boat while leading a local race, much to the amusement of my staff and fellow racers. The Patuxent 17.5 is a less extreme version of the Patuxent for those of us who don't paddle flat-out most of the time. Both versions are of hard-chine construction with minimal fiberglass reinforcement and 3 mm decks to save weight. Obviously, neither version is as rugged as a touring boat. The Patuxent 19.5 is 19 feet, 6 inches long, with a beam of 21 inches and a weight of 34 pounds. The 17.5 is, you guessed it, 17 feet, 6 inches long, with a 22-inch beam and a weight of 34 pounds.

An ultralight flatwater kayak, the pretty little Severn weighs only 26 pounds.

THE SEVERN KAYAK

The Severn is a 26-pound flatwater kayak built using an unusual method called compounded plywood. Two carefully shaped panels are bent and twisted to form a round-bottomed hull. This is a fast way to build an ultralight boat, but the process is exacting and not intuitive. The 14-foot, 7-inch Severn is not particularly fast, but it moves with little effort. It's a low-volume boat best suited for paddlers under 180 pounds; total capacity is about 210 pounds. Plans and building instructions for the Severn are in *The New Kayak Shop*.

TRED AVON KAYAK

The Tred Avon is an older design for a medium-volume, coastal-touring double based on the old Cape Charles design. It has considerable rocker and is quite light

for a double. I would say that the newer Chesapeake 21 is a better all-around double, but if you want a kayak with less volume and wetted-surface area, this would be a good choice. It can be built from only four 4-by-8 sheets of 4 mm plywood in either an open or a two-cockpit configuration. Its LOA (length overall) is 21 feet, beam is 29 inches, and weight comes in at 55 pounds. I've also designed a triple version with a smaller center cockpit designed primarily for children.

WEST RIVER KAYAKS

The West River 164 and 162 are strong, stable touring boats for paddlers who prefer a multi-chine or rounded-hull shape. The 162 and 164 share the same basic hull shape. But the 164 has a higher freeboard and more room for gear and large feet. It is

ABOVE: *The West River kayaks are modern multi-chine sea kayaks.* RIGHT: *The bolt-on SailRig turns any kayak into a fast trimaran.*

really very roomy for its length. Both models are 16 feet, 3 inches long, have a 24-inch beam, and weigh about 40 pounds.

The West River 180 is a very fast and rugged multi-chine hull kayak for the experienced paddler. The West River 180's waterline length is almost 17½ feet to provide enough speed when we're feeling strong. A beam of 22 inches in a hull with firm bilges provides reasonable initial stability while still retaining a fairly low wetted-surface area. Its dimensions of 18 feet by 22 inches are the maximum length and minimum beam allowed in the "touring class" in many sea kayak races. *The New Kayak Shop* contains plans and building instructions for the West River 180.

THE SAILRIG

The SailRig is not a boat in itself, but rather an outrigger that transforms a canoe or kayak into a stable sailing trimaran. It can be rigged for sailing or dismantled for cartopping in about 15 minutes. When mounted on the right boat, the

Although kayaking is the best way to explore, a rowing shell such as this Oxford Shell provides wonderful exercise.

SailRig is faster than many small sailboats. With two compounded-plywood hulls, and two 10-foot laminated outriggers, as well as aluminum mounting brackets and a leeboard, the SailRig may be more work to build than the boat it's mounted on. The mast is an aircraft-grade aluminum tube, and the sails are available from Chesapeake Light Craft. Of course, you must mount a foot-operated sea kayak–type rudder on your boat to steer.

OXFORD SHELL

There is, in my opinion, no form of exercise superior to rowing a sliding-seat boat. Sculling works both the upper and lower body, builds aerobic capacity, and is a relatively injury-free sport. The Oxford Shell is an all-around recreational shell. It is intended for training in smooth water, though it will handle chop of up to a foot

or so. It is actually simpler to build than the Sassafras canoes. The Oxford Shell uses an Alden or a Piantedosi drop-in rowing unit, so you have only to build the hull; all the rigging can be installed (or removed) in less than a minute. This makes cartopping and storage much easier than with most shells of this level of performance.

ANNAPOLIS WHERRY

The Annapolis Wherry, a 17-foot, 9-inch fast rowing boat, is built using the LapStitch stitch-and-glue construction method. Although the Annapolis Wherry can be rowed in normal fixed-seat fashion, it is at its best when powered by a sliding-seat rig. This is the boat I use most often; I keep one at my dock and try to get out for a row every couple of days. Over the past two years, I've put hundreds of miles under its keel without a single complaint. If your aim is to get a serious workout, and you live near open, choppy water, this is the ideal boat.

JIMMY SKIFF

It has often been said that good skiffs are among the easiest boats to build, yet the hardest to design. I think that the Jimmy Skiff, my adaptation of the classic Chesapeake Bay crabbing skiff, is a "good skiff." It makes a fine sailing and rowing craft. At 13 feet and 95 pounds, it is small and light enough to cartop, yet it will carry a family of four. The Jimmy Skiff's simple sprit sailing rig can be set up in about five minutes. I can think of no better boat in which to learn how to sail. Of course, you might prefer to leave the sailing rig off, ship some oars, and go fishing or crabbing

The Annapolis Wherry is my favorite rowing boat. It is fast, stable, seaworthy, and beautiful.

as generations of watermen here on the Chesapeake have done in their skiffs.

The Jimmy Skiff is based on traditional Chesapeake Bay sailing skiffs. It's fun under sail or under oar power.

Resources

BOOKS ABOUT BOATBUILDING AND CANOE BUILDING

Gougeon Brothers. *The Gougeon Brothers on Boat Construction: Wood & WEST SYSTEM Materials*. New rev. (4th) ed. Bay City MI: Gougeon Brothers, 1985. The bible of wood-epoxy construction.

Hazen, David. *The Stripper's Guide to Canoe-Building*. Larkspur CA: Tamal Vista Publications, 1996.

Hill, Thomas J. *Ultralight Boatbuilding*. Camden ME: International Marine, 1987. Glued lapstrake canoe and skiff construction.

Moores, Ted, and Merilyn Mohr. *Canoecraft*. Toronto: Camden House Publishing, 1983. Strip construction.

Stelmok, Jerry, and Roland Thurlow. *The Wood and Canvas Canoe*. Gardiner ME: Tilbury House, 1987.

Wittman, Rebecca J. *Brightwork: The Art of Finishing Wood*. Camden ME: International Marine, 1990. Looking for the ultimate finish.

PERIODICALS

Boatbuilder
P.O. Box 3000
Denville NJ 07834
Most articles focus on building large boats, but many of the techniques translate.

Fine Woodworking
Taunton Press
P.O. Box 5506
Newtown CT 06470
Although largely devoted to furniture making and tool reviews, this magazine is well written and will interest any woodworker.

Messing about in Boats
29 Burley St.
Wenham MA 01984
Most articles in this iconoclastic little bi-weekly are about homebuilt boats, weird designs, and getting out on the water on the cheap. It's fun and inexpensive, and I urge you to subscribe.

Notes from Our Shop
1805 George Ave.
Annapolis MD 21401
This free newsletter from Chesapeake Light Craft contains articles and shop tips related to building small boats.

WoodenBoat
P.O. Box 78
Brooklin ME 04616
This thick and glossy bimonthly is chock-full with well-written articles on all aspects of using, designing, and building wooden craft. *WoodenBoat* is simply the best magazine on the subject of boat-building.

SUPPLIERS

These are companies that I have done business with and can recommend or that have been recommended to me by friends or by other boatbuilders. Other suppliers can be found by looking through the ads in *WoodenBoat* magazine.

Boulter Plywood Corp.
24 Broadway
Somerville MA 02145
617-666-1340
Plywood.

Chesapeake Light Craft
1805 George Ave.
Annapolis, MD 21401
410-267-0137
www.clcboats.com
Plans and kits for the boats in this book, plywood, epoxy, hardware, and accessories.

Chesapeake Marine Fasteners
10 Willow St.
Annapolis MD 21401
410-266-9332
Fasteners.

Clark Craft
16 Aqua Ln.
Tonawanda NY 14150
716-873-2640
Some canoe plans.

Flounder Bay Boat Lumber
1019 3rd St.
Anacortes WA 98221
800-228-4691
Plywood.

Harbor Sales Co.
1000 Harbor Ct.
Sudlersville MD 21668
800-345-1712
Probably the largest marine plywood distributor in North America.

Jamestown Distributors
28 Narragansett Ave.
Jamestown RI 02835
800-423-0030
Epoxy, hardware, fiberglass tape, and a wide range of boatbuilding supplies and tools.

Japan Woodworker Company
1731 Clement Ave.
Alameda CA 94501
800-537-7820
Japanese woodworking tools.

Lee Valley Tools Ltd.
P.O. Box 1780
Ogdensburg NY 13669
800-871-8185
Hand tools and woodworking supplies.

M. L. Condon Co.
260 Ferris Ave.
White Plains NY 10603
914-946-4111
Lumber and plywood.

Noahs Marine Supplies
54 Six Point Rd.
Toronto ON
CANADA M8Z 2X2
416-232-0522
Boatbuilding supplies.

Red Hill Corp.
P.O. Box 4234
Gettysburg PA 17325
800-822-4003
Bulk sandpaper and related supplies.

Tool Crib of the North
P.O. Box 14930
Grand Forks ND 58208
800-635-5140
Power and hand tools.

Garrett Wade
161 Ave. of the Americas
New York NY 10013
800-221-2942
Tools.

WoodenBoat Store
P.O. Box 78
Brooklin ME 04616
207-359-4651
Small-boat plans, books, a few tools.

Woodworkers Supply
1108 North Glenn Rd.
Casper WY 82601
800-645-9292
Woodworking tools and supplies.

BOATBUILDERS

In case you prefer to have one of my designs custom-built.

Bill Thomas
P.O. Box 384
Stevensville, MD 21666
410-643-7597

Sharpening Tools

One of the first things I do when teaching a boatbuilding class is show my students how to sharpen their block planes and other edged tools. Watching a roomful of students struggling with dull tools is too much to bear; boatbuilding should be fun, and sharp, well-adjusted tools are a pleasure to use.

I prefer to sharpen on a Japanese waterstone. I think it is easier to use and leaves a better edge than an oilstone or Arkansas stone. A combination waterstone with a 1,000-grit surface on one side and a 6,000-grit surface on the other is perfect for sharpening woodworking tools or even kitchen knives. These stones use water as a lubricant and should be soaked for a few hours before use. I store my stone in a water-filled plastic container. Here I describe sharpening a plane's blade, or iron, but most tools are sharpened the same way.

First flatten the back; the back of the iron makes half the sharp edge, so this is important. Splash some water onto the coarse side of the stone and lay the iron, back face down, on it. Sharpen the iron by pushing it up and down the stone in a circular motion. Use the entire stone, splash more water on it frequently, and check often to see whether the back is smooth and flat. This may take some time if this is a

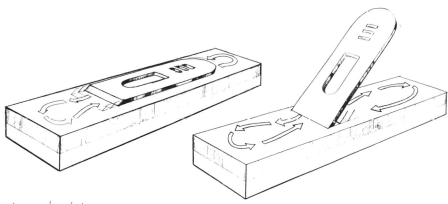

Sharpening a plane's iron.

new tool; tool factories do a poor job of sharpening blades these days. When you see that the stone has made contact with the entire back of the iron (look at the sheen), sharpen for 3 more minutes on the fine side of the stone.

Now sharpen the front. Hold the iron against the coarse side of the stone so that it rests on its bevel. Rock the blade slightly to get a feel for when it's resting squarely on the bevel. Alternately, use a sharpening jig that holds the iron at the correct angle; serious woodworkers will find a jig indispensable. Move the blade back and forth on the stone, making a long oval circuit. Keep your fingers close to the bevel and press down gently. Be careful to keep the iron at a constant angle, with the bevel flat on the stone. When the entire bevel has been sharpened (again, look at the sheen), repeat for 1 minute, or 20 up-and-down strokes, on the fine side. Now draw your fingernail down the back of the edge. You should feel a tiny burr, or "wire," made by the thin metal edge bent back in the sharpening process. Lay the blade on its back again and pull it down the stone once to remove the wire. Finally, dry the iron. If you did everything right, you can almost shave with this edge. Once the iron is true and sharp, sharpen it often; the process will take only a few minutes.

If you don't have the temperament to hand-sharpen tools and can afford an electric waterstone sharpener, don't hesitate to get one. My little Wen electric sharpener is one of my most appreciated tools.

METRIC CONVERSION TABLE

1 inch	2.54 centimeters
1 inch	25.4 millimeters
1 foot	0.3 meters
1 yard	0.914 meters
1 pound	0.45 kilograms
1 ounce	28.35 grams
1 gallon	3.785 kilograms
1 knot	1.85 kilometers/hour
1 mile/hour	1.609 kilometers/hour
1 nautical mile	1.85 kilometers
°F	°C × 1.8 + 32
°C	(°F−32) × 0.555

INDEX

Page numbers in **bold** refer to pages with illustrations. The appendices are not indexed.